The Tao of Science

by
R. G. H. SIU

The Tao of Science

An Essay
on Western Knowledge
and
Eastern Wisdom

The M.I.T. Press
Massachusetts Institute of Technology
Cambridge, Massachusetts

To Irene I-lien Siu

Preface

THE AMERICAN WAY of life is a doing way. It is not characteristically a reflecting way, nor a subtle way. Deep meditation, painstaking
analysis, and meticulous planning are but preludes to action. The
instinctive guiding axiom is seldom: "If you don't know what to do,
do *nothing*." It is instead: "If you don't know what to do, *do* something."

Doing has built the gigantic American industrial complex. Doing
has raised the American standard of living to an unrivaled level. Doing
has brought about the vast array of matériel that flows from America to
distant lands throughout the world.

Yet sheer doing is not living. The former is but a mechanical manifestation of the latter. Living is grounded more in the resilient subtleties
behind the action emerging from the imperceptible recesses of the thinking man, the praying man, and even the sleeping man.

Since it is living for which we are searching—good living, that is,
leaving aside the definition of "good" for the moment—many of us have
reached out between our hurried activities for some proper orientation
of living to doing. The current trend seems to becloud the issue of life
with the issue of action. The eminent American philosophers William
James and John Dewey very capably seized upon the dilemma decades
ago. But even these great thinkers were overwhelmed with the American
posture of doing. Their philosophies became the basis of more doing.

Today, then, we find the action wheel revolving ever faster. Somehow reflecting minds merely add lubricant to the bearings. This seems to have been the product of American philosophy upon the American scene. Yet it is not entirely unexpected. How else would a doing mind influence a doing system?

It might have been a different story had the analyses been made against the reflective tradition of the Orient. The life of an executive—that focus of American doing—may well be enriched by invoking the wisdom of sages of another clime and age. This book represents a case study (note: typical of the American doing approach) in this direction. [The management of organized research has been selected for treatment.]

A discussion of science and organized research is timely for the twentieth century. The spirit of inquiry occupies a position of dominance in our culture. Great things were expected from this approach to life when it first became a matter of common practice following the Renaissance. This interrogation of the meaning of existence and the attendant refusal to accept the literal tutelage of the Scriptures stimulated the rapid advancement of science. It also led to noble literature, great paintings, and other marvelous human creations. Yet the feeling of inadequacy in the deeper and universal riddles of life remained. The absolutes have not been found. Man's ability to ask questions has outstripped his ability to answer.

Science has been a prime force behind this inquiring movement. [As science continues to exert ever-increasing influence on man's ways, we should reassess her role and behavior to see "what has gone wrong," so to speak, that she has failed to produce the expected millennium, but on the contrary has brought on growing apprehension as to her ultimate value to society.] With scientific investigations being organized as they are today, there is probably no more appropriate place to begin this introspection than with the managers of research.

Let us, therefore, observe and analyze the behavior of professors, deans, directors of research, vice-presidents in charge of research, and presidents of foundations and technological enterprises. Let us see how the old Oriental sages, were they alive, would advise these modern executives of creative talents.

What are the philosophic and aesthetic features of their daily decisions? Do the fashions and foibles of science do violence to the beauty of nature and the reality of life? [Has the scientific method, which has served man well in his material advancement during the past three hundred years, reached the point of diminishing effectiveness for humane progress?] How should the implications of these soul-searching questions affect the management of research?

As a director of research, I, too, find myself contemplating the same issues. In some ways the deliberations have been especially perplexing. My childhood was influenced by the classical ways of the Orient. As a youngster I asked my share of questions. The invariable answers followed: " 'Tis as 'tis." At times my father would use a variant of the same theme: "*After* you have consumed ten hundredweights of salt, *then* you will understand." Timely acceptance of the given seemed a desirable way of life. Wisdom coupled it with that silent understanding which did not require explanation.

The early schooling was chimeric. In the first part of the day, I studied the sciences of the West; I learned that progress is fed by the constant passion for change. In the late afternoon I pored over Mencius and the other Chinese classics; I memorized the story extolling the virtues of the merchant who for thirty years sold identical wares at the same location without ever varying his price.

As time went on, I continued along the Occidental path of science. The Oriental schooling and parental lectures on the harmony of life, the beauty of contentment, and the ineffability of nature were left far behind. I slogged along a narrow specialty, published scientific driblets, lectured to scientific audiences, and moved within a convivial coterie of scientific confreres. Through chance circumstances (good fortune in the judgment of some friends and a pity in the eyes of others) I was shunted into the managerial line of advancement. Again I ploddingly went from group leader to laboratory supervisor to director of research. I became an executive.

When the distraught days—familiar to every executive—brought with them the puzzlement of immiscible goods and the straining of patience in perennial crises, the almost forgotten Oriental lessons would come bobbing to the rescue with increasing frequency. At first, the essence of Oriental classics and that of Western science did not appear compatible. The synthesis into unitary action seemed impossible. Nevertheless, the oscillating current of thought between the two poles kept me intrigued with the possibility of injecting the temperamental advantages of the ancient Oriental diffusive steadiness into the pointed fast-moving technicism of the modern West. Relevant thoughts are presented in the chapters which follow.

In truth I must confess that I have not yet consumed the ten hundredweights of salt, which my good and wise father had prescribed as the prerequisite to enlightenment. I would therefore like to ask the indulgence of my honorable and learned readers, especially the professional philosopher into whose familiar provinces I have wandered at times in the telling of my simple and practical story.

R. G. H. SIU

Washington, D. C.
September 1957

Acknowledgments

THE AUTHOR WISHES TO ACKNOWLEDGE the kind permission of the following for the use of excerpts from various works.

Alfred A. Knopf: Arthur Waley's *Translations from the Chinese*.

Dodd, Mead and Company: Rupert Brooke's poem, *The Dead*.

Harcourt, Brace and Company: Carl Sandburg's poem, *The People, Yes*.

Houghton Mifflin Company: Ralph Waldo Emerson's poem, *Brahma*.

Little, Brown and Company: Emily Dickinson's poem, *I Never Saw a Moor*.

Mrs. Carlotta Monterey O'Neill: Eugene O'Neill's play, *Long Day's Journey into Night*.

New Directions: Thomas Merton's *Seeds of Contemplation*.

Random House: Lin Yu-tang's *The Wisdom of Lao-tze*.

The Hudson Review (Spring issue, 1955): Kuangchi Chang's article, *Poetry of the Sung Dynasty*.

The John Day Company: Lin Yu-tang's *The Gay Genius*.

The Macmillan Company: Fung Yu-lan's *A Short History of Chinese Philosophy*.

W. W. Norton and Company: Marcus Long's *The Spirit of Philosophy*.

Contents

Contents

A

Perspective

of

Scientific

Progress

Chapter 1

Science Speeds on Unabashed

THE ADVANCEMENT OF SCIENCE continues at a terrifying pace.

A tiny fork of light was photographed in January 1939 in a cloistered German laboratory. Within the short span of six and a half years the joint efforts of two other nations parlayed this innocent observation into the most awesome weapon of death. A single atomic bomb obliterated a hundred thousand lives and destroyed eight square miles of a fourth community. And scarcely ten years later, threats shuttled across the international waters involving still a fifth country that intercontinental missiles thousands of times more devastating were in the offing.

Scientists are debating whether their brain child intends to leave any earth for them to inhabit, not to say investigate and understand. They are recalling the tragedy of the mythical Greek hunter Actaeon, who accidentally saw Artemis, the goddess of chastity, bathing on Mount Cithaeron. For that he was changed into a stag, to be chased by his own fifty hounds until they killed him. Is there any moral in the story for scientists?—men are beginning to ask.

And all the while, the Devil's words to Shaw's Don Juan keep taunting in the background: "And is Man any the less destroying himself for all this boasted brain of his? . . . and I tell you that in the arts of life man invents nothing; but in the art of death he outdoes Nature herself. . . . This marvellous force of Life of which you boast is a force of Death. Man measures his strength by his destructiveness."

The Devil's distortion is a sly one. The scientist must join Don Juan in his "Pshaw!" He can point to the eighteen tons of material spawned by his fecund genius, which are annually consumed by the average American. For a specific example, he need look no farther than his medicine chest. Concurrently with the engineering of that dreadful implement of death, the very same two powers joined hands to develop the most effective instrument of life that the world of medicine has ever known. Penicillin and the dozen other antibiotics were transformed from test tube curiosities to life-saving prescriptions within the same period of time.

Meanwhile, impatient and inquisitive, science sent her scouts into the dark depths of the ocean and the far reaches of the sky. At the midpoint of the twentieth century they have sounded 35,000 feet below the surface of the seas and ranged to 90,000 above. Where they could not personally touch and observe, they extended their hands through 300 miles of heavens by speedy rockets, their eyes to 10 billion trillion miles by powerful lenses.

If nature attempts to conceal her tiny secrets, science bares them publicly with magnifications of five millionfold. Neither the porcupine nor the mosquito can keep its love life to itself any longer. Scientists peep into their private familiarities and delight in detailed descriptions in lectures and papers. If God's molecular gifts are too bulky for human utility, science chops them into little pieces of useful chemicals. If the natural bits are too small, science joins them together into larger units. If the Thanksgiving turkey is too large, a small one is bred. If seeds are not wanted in fruits, seedless varieties are developed. Not satisfied with man's mundane three-dimensional world, science conjures up four- and six-dimensional phantasms.

The curiosity of science and her bent for innovation seem uncontrollable. She pries into every heavenly nook and earthly cranny. She respects neither the ancient sanctity of tombs nor the caressing intimacies of boudoirs.

Science speeds on unabashed!

Chapter 2

Historical Forces behind Modern Science

NOTHING SEEMS TO DETER modern science from plunging into areas where even "angels fear to tread." Nothing seems to restrain her audacious momentum. How did she get this way? Let us peer into her lineage and heritage. Perhaps we can find some clues.

To begin with, science did not conjure forth herself phoenix-like out of her own ashes. Nor did she spring like Athena full-grown from the teachings of Bacon, Newton, and Locke, suddenly dispelling the darkness of the earlier world. [Science was the natural consequence of a long cultural progress extending thousands upon thousands of years.] Her birth coincided with the creation of Adam and Eve. Her development paralleled the intellectual refinement of their descendants. Her modern inventions are the culminations of infinite numbers of small increments of interacting and cumulative advancements.

Man's bodily evolution reached its present form about twenty-five thousand years ago. Since then there has been a continuous unfolding of his mental capacities. Even at that time the Cro-Magnons in France were already paying attention to life far beyond the bare necessities of food. Spirited inscriptions of women and animals were being made on the walls of their caves. Expressive creativity was an early human trait.

We observe increasing skills as primitive man progressed beyond the simple life of hunting with crude stone and bone implements and of gathering ready foods from nature. He gradually learned to exert greater control over his sources of subsistence through the cultivation of plants and the breeding of animals. In place of nomadic garden culture, he exploited the natural irrigation afforded by rains and floods. By this means the same patches of land were cultivated repeatedly. Cattle, sheep, goats, and swine were associated with these crude farms. This was followed by the growth of communities with a surplus of food for the support of the other workers, who were drawn from the food producers. There were the miners, the smelters, the craftsmen, the transporters, the clerks, the officials, and the priests. Already in those days of eight thousand years ago, considerable know-how had been acquired in the industrial arts. Occupational specialization had already begun.

With the availability of cheap tools the way was opened for a rapid expansion of agriculture and technology. Between 6000 and 3000 B. C. the inventions were revolutionary. The plow was devised; the wheeled cart was in use on land and the sailboat on water; the inclined plane and lever were common implements. Copper ores were smelted; bronze was alloyed; bricks and pottery were fired. Canals and ditches were dug; grains were fermented; orchards were planted. There were the arch and the seal. At the same time a systematic urban life became clearly outlined. There was an accurate solar calendar; eclipses were predicted. There were adequate methods of accounting and measuring. There was a definite recording of information and transmission of knowledge from one individual to another and from one generation to the next. Discoveries of that period are unrivaled in their impact on human progress. Even today's science cannot match them in fundamental importance to the basic well-being of man.

Although the contributions during the next 3000 years were not as fundamental as in the previous trimillennia, they were nonetheless notable. Four of the more important were: the decimal notation (about 2000 B. C.), the industrial method of smelting iron (1400 B. C.), a truly alphabetic script (1300 B. C.), and aqueducts for supplying water to urban centers (700 B. C.).

Theoretical and speculative thinking was also pursued with vigor during those early days. Babylonian cuneiform tablets and Egyptian

6

papyrus containing calculations of areas and volumes date back to 2000 B. C. *The Canonical Book of Changes,* the *Yi-ching,* written in 1200 B. C., described the Chinese hypothesis on transformations in nature resulting from the interactions of the polar contraries, the Ying and the Yang. The concept of the elemental composition of matter had been recorded a thousand years earlier in the *Canonical Book of Records,* the *Shu-ching.* In the latter treatise matter consisted of the five elements: metal, wood, earth, fire, and water.

More elaborate systems were developed by the Hindus. Their religious texts of the period contained references to nine universal constituents of nature: the tangible atomic substances of water, fire, air, and earth; the infinite, eternal, nonatomic ether; the nonmaterial time-space; the individual soul; the universal soul; and the Manas, which is the medium of sensing and understanding for the individual soul.

The Greeks, too, had their share of great abstract thinkers. Thales, for example, had predicted the eclipse of 585 B. C. A theory of biological evolution of man was advanced over two millennia before Darwin by Anaximander around 560 B. C. The use of geometrical analyses was begun by Pythagoras in his astronomical studies around 520 B. C. In contrast to Thales, who thought that everything was made of water, Heraclitus (ca. 500 B. C.) proposed that fire is the primordial element. The atomic construction of matter was stated over two millennia before Dalton by Democritus in 420 B. C. His contemporary Socrates, who allegedly learnt much as a youth from the erudite Parmenides, was followed by the philosophers Plato (ca. 428–348 B. C.) and Aristotle (384–322 B. C.).

It becomes readily apparent from these excerpts of human attainments before Christ that the urge toward material and intellectual advancement is not novel with modern science. This is as old as man. Neither is the fruitful realization of its power an accomplishment unique to today's scientific society. This too is as old as man. Let us now scan the periods after Christ and note the changing modes of thought which finally led to the maturity and vitality of modern science. Santayana depicted the Western transformation in an elegant fashion by contrasting the writings of representative poets from three eras: Lucretius (ca. 99–55 B. C.), Dante (1265–1321), and Goethe (1749–1832).

In the pre-Socratic days Greece was pervaded with a materialism in

7

natural science and a humanism in ethics. The universe is one totality. The harmonious components all mutually support and enhance each other according to a master plan of constant redistribution of the elemental atoms. Old things are perpetually being converted into new ones. Human life, too, belongs to this cycle. Human history is thus equated with the story of nature. Emphasis is laid on the happiness of man on earth. Lucretius gave poetic eloquence to this frame of mind: We are to eat, drink, and be merry within the artistic confines of good health.

After a thousand years, supernaturalism became the dominant theme. An overriding religious influence impressed itself on all minds and institutions. The world no longer is the destiny of man. It is the tempting ground of the devil whose wits are pitted against those of man in a test of man's worthiness for a future reward in eternity. On earth happiness is impossible. Man's freedom is not only a source of good; it is also a source of evil. His ultimate joy lies in union with God in the heaven to come. Life therefore becomes his opportunity to prove his merits through a patient acceptance of earthly pains and discomforts. All contemplation revolves around the aspirations of the soul. Dante, of course, was the sensitive poet of this age.

Gradually the Roman and the Teutonic worlds generated a reaction against the dogmatism of the Scholastic institutions. Romanticism began to gain ascendancy five hundred years later. People relished the savor of unfettered imagination and asserted their individualism. They felt their freedom as a way out of their pent-up perplexity, and a new vista of life unfolded before them. They turned from the Bible to knowledge, to wealth, to art, to sports, to escapade after escapade. Their appetite for flitting successions of new activity was insatiable, and when the object of each activity was at last attained, it emerged an empty mirage. It escaped their grasp and left their souls aching for new games. Each intermission merely set off a new chain of restlessness. Entranced by the spectacle of the swift pursuit in a life of eternal failures, they soon lost themselves in the chase for the sake of the chase. This, it turned out, was the best prophylaxis for ennui and boredom. Goethe painted the tragic picture in *Faust*.

The marked political changes of the seventeenth century also fostered a fertile intellectual environment for science. As feudal institutions began to decay, there was a transfer of business from the country to the city. People became free of their divinely anointed rulers. They were organized into states, which were believed to exist for the satisfaction of human needs and human ideals. The importance of the individual in his freedom of opinion permeated the times. A newly found independence and initiative of thought resulted.

Together with this ranging of the mind, there had been a thoroughgoing conviction in Medieval Europe that every detailed occurrence in nature was traceable to a demonstrable cause. This was the natural extension of the rationality of God. The universe was a casting of the Master Plan. This outgrowth of medieval theology generated a receptive attitude toward the rationality of science, which was spearheaded by the rise of mathematics and rationalism of the later Middle Ages. Science felt certain that reason can illumine the darkness of human puzzlement. She will not require an appeal to Holy Writ. She will rely on her own verifiable concepts and observations.

The emergence of modern science in the seventeenth century was accompanied by an explosive brilliance of contributions in all phases of human creation. The century was ushered in by the publication of Gilbert's pioneering work on the magnet in 1600. This was quickly followed by Shakespeare's early edition of *Hamlet* in 1604 and Cervantes' *Don Quixote* in 1605. Soon Rembrandt and Milton were to be born. The invention of the telescope took place in 1608 and Kepler's pronouncements of his first two laws of planetary motion in 1609. Galileo was launching his trail-blazing experiments. El Greco was in his prime. Rubens was beginning his career. In 1628 Harvey advanced his theory of the circulation of blood. Descartes published his *Discourse on Method* in 1637. This was just 10, 5, and 3 years after the births of the chemist Boyle, the architect Wren, and the philosopher Spinoza, respectively, and 5 years before the birth of the physicist Newton.

Undisputed dominance in the field of the intellect was finally established by science when she allied herself with industrial and economic interests. Her willingness to forsake scholastic for material objectives attracted larger subsidies that resulted in a rapid expansion of scientific effort. Business provided not only financial support but also concrete, achievable incentives. In the medieval days, God's world was in His power alone. Man was helpless before pestilences, drought, and famine.

Man could only hope that these symptoms of God's wrath would be alleviated through his humility and good works. In his new frame of mind, however, man became rapidly dissatisfied with the gifts of nature. Incited by commerce and industry, Promethean man forged science into an instrument of change. Her principal task is to modify the contents of the cosmos according to man's designs and wants. The medieval bastions for the search of God's truth tottered from the assault of utility.

Utilitarianism focused the expansive view of eternity and universal generalities into intensely localized particulars. Human achievement in the concrete became the goal of those professing to the social good. This was the modern phantasmagorical substitute in lieu of the pious resignation to the unfathomable ways of the Lord. Not only science but also labor, art, and at times even religion came to be looked upon as means to sensuous enjoyment. Learning was no longer a passive process of ethereal reflection but an active, terrestrial, and practical pursuit.

The broad base for the popularity of modern science was thus laid. For the first time man found a versatile outlet for his multitudinous desires and diverse ends. Science was the magic wand for all human passions. It worked for saints and sinners, young and old, proud and humble. It had no preferences, no morals, no feelings. The scholar found science useful in tracing the majesty and the beauty of the Lord's creation. The humble looked to science in contemplating man's feeble insignificance in the uncovered vastness. The vain exploited science to garnish themselves with honors and adulation. The theologian used science as a convincing tool for the confirmation of God's ways. The atheist employed science as the basis for his godless world. The general waged war, with science providing his implements of destruction. The pacifist emphasized science as an agent to world peace through the perpetuation of material abundance. The businessman paid generous bonuses to science as the ideal servant who gets things done, makes money, and never asks questions. The artist was fascinated by the aesthetic patterns that kept unfolding before the successive explorations of science.

The patronage of science in the Western world was universal as she stood on the threshold of the nineteenth century. With such auspicious support, her tremendous progress during the ensuing years was a foregone conclusion.

Chapter 3

Specialists and Research Teams

IN THIS CHAPTER WE SHALL OUTLINE the main factors that contributed to the sweeping growth of science in her pursuit of utilitarianism. There was an intensity of specialization, driving deep salients into the frontiers of knowledge. There was an increase in facilities for training the required specialists. There was an improvement in communications, which made possible the fertile exchange of ideas. There was the practice of organized research, which fused relevant skills into concerted and directional action. These were the chief elements that fed the breeder reaction in the ever-expanding pile of science.

Before the Middle Ages, the scope of the scholar was all encompassing. The leaders of society sought a comprehension of God's total universe. Increase in one's understanding was directed toward the simultaneous movement along the entire front of knowledge. Such an approach had serious drawbacks. First, it provided little concentration of energy at any point for a penetrating thrust. Second, it limited the number of successful participants, since there were few individuals with the requisite breadth of mind. Third, it lacked direction and consequently was limited in utility. It did not take science long to recognize that for maximum effect a new approach must be perfected. The search quickly led to a division of intellectual labor.

Specialization accorded considerable advantages to the individual. Inasmuch as the horizon of possible knowledge is unlimited, the number of areas open to his selection is very large. Under such a scheme most people, talented or mediocre in native ability, are capable of at least restricted excellence. To gain the esteem of the world as a learned authority one needs only to persevere in a circumscribed field of interest which is carefully selected to fit his temperament and is relatively shorn of competitors. This enables the generally inept but concretely capable, who comprise a goodly number in the world, to contribute significantly to science and at the same time to gain considerable recognition. The universal scholar gradually became a dodo of the past; the narrow specialist rapidly gained ascendancy.

Recurring attempts have been made to stem the advances of the "intellectual splitters." [The philosophically-minded argued that the specialist surveys too skimpy a perspective of the world. What one should acquire is a familiarity with a wider array of disciplines in order to develop a broader cognizance of life and an integrated knowledge of nature.] Many educators have modified teaching curricula for the development of generalists.

These movements have never realized much momentum, however. They were unable to offer compensating rewards to offset the alluring successes of the specialists. Philanthropic foundations committed large financial resources to the advancement of confined disciplines. Governments established grants toward the same end. Prizes and honors were dangled before the eyes of students who would join the race in the natural sciences. Always the greatness of specialists is acclaimed: Galileo, Boyle, Newton, Darwin, Gibbs, Morgan, Einstein. The Leonardo da Vincis, the Benjamin Franklins, the Johann Wolfgang von Goethes were considered departures from the norm of true scientists. Against these incentives for specialization few but the starry-eyed would wander off the fashionable path. How many of our professionals would follow Albert Schweitzer's example of deliberately reducing his specialized advancement in order to add stature to his life in its entirety? By the beginning of the twentieth century, the experts of the particulars commanded by far the greater respect. No matter how valuable the aesthetic sensibilities that were passed over, hard cash and fame now followed the specialized elaborator.

Growth in science was also nurtured in other ways. Thinking is the successive refinement of ideas. One of the most effective media is the presentation of thought for evaluation, for criticism, for recasting in more useful templates, and for extension into novel areas. For this reason facility in the transmission of an idea from one individual to another affects the progress of science to a large degree. Any activity which hastens this interchange provides a significant impetus. The influence of printing is well recognized. In 1954, in the United States, 12,000 new titles of books were published. Half a billion copies were sold. There are approximately 3000 technical journals in the world. Over a million articles on technical subjects are printed each year. Proper acknowledgment has been repeatedly paid to Gutenberg.

The contributions of other events, however, have been taken for granted. The discovery of America by Columbus is a simple example. It provided new settings and challenges against which ideas can be tested. In the United States the frontier moved rapidly from the ships under Christopher Newport that sailed into Hampton Roads in 1607 to found Jamestown to the arrival of John Bidwell's first emigrant train to Oregon in 1841. Networks of communications connected the growing settlements. There were the famous trails blazed westward from St. Louis: the overland trails of Fremont, Pike, Lewis and Clark, the Santa Fe, Mormon, Oregon, and California trails. Around the turn of the century these developed rapidly into the great railroad systems, the empires of Gould, Harriman, Hill, Morgan, and Vanderbilt.

With the extension of transportation facilities, peoples once far separated became capable of close contact. As the speed of communication mounted the frequency of scientific meetings increased correspondingly. In 1954 there were about 1400 technical groups in the United States among which research data and concepts were bantered, argued, deliberated upon, and, in essence, improved.

Another strong stimulus to science was the groupings of specialized talents into teams. When it became evident that one mind could not master all skills across the board of knowledge, the employment of a cooperative approach was quite natural. Industry soon recognized the power of a skilfully directed attack toward a specific purpose and became its stoutest patron.

The president of the largest chemical company in the world reasoned during the Depression that it was more important to carry on research than to pay dividends. Sixty per cent of the sales of his company in 1970 will probably grow from products still in their infancy today. This is the general industrial picture. It has been estimated that scientific discoveries account for 95 per cent of the current income for the mining industry, 90 per cent for manufacturing, 85 for commerce, 80 for agriculture, 50 for forestry, and 100 for transportation. In the thirty-year interval between 1920 and 1950 the number of industrial laboratories in the United States rose tenfold to 6000. The national expenditure in research and development increased over twentyfold from 166 million dollars in 1930 to 3.7 billion in 1952. Today there are about 180,000 researchers in the United States, nine tenths of whom are subsidized through organized programs. These figures are impressive indices of the recent growth of organized research.

The demand for increasing numbers of specialists was met by a streamlining of the training methods. The production of specialists in universities thus became an organized effort in itself. With the separation of the Ecole Polytechnique from the Ecole des Beaux-Arts at the end of the eighteenth century, the modern educational dichotomy between science and art became firmly set. Expert scientists began a serious program of research apprenticeship for students at the Ecole Polytechnique. Since then there followed a rapid increase of training centers. The rate can be gained from a count of the number of universities, technical schools, and theological institutions in the Western world. From the fifteenth to the nineteenth centuries inclusive the numbers ran: 57, 98, 129, 180, 603. In 1954 the total enrollment of students in the 170,000 schools of the United States ran to 38,000,000 or 24 per cent of the total population.

In the field of research, universities are looked upon primarily as strong centers for individual investigations. Yet even here the practice of a team approach has been steadily gaining ground. This trend is reflected in the type of authorship of papers being published. Eighty-five per cent of the articles in *Science,* for example, were contributed by single authors in 1921 and 15 per cent by two co-authors. Three decades later single authors accounted for only 35 per cent; co-authors of two comprised 38 per cent; the other 27 per cent stemmed from joint authorships involving three to eight persons. In the laboratory academicians band together in research groups. In the classroom they sponsor cooperative courses and share teaching loads. The character of education is rapidly becoming a reverberating echo of the fashion of current society in which bigness has assumed a mantle of virtue and organized effort is the quickest way to it.

Thus it is that the smoothly operating research teams are piling up the impressive scores in today's science and technology. The individual experimenter seems to be hemmed in on all sides. He finds retreat in the lofty towers of abstract theories and pioneering adventures. But even there his friends are insisting on making it a party, bringing with them tasty meat and delicious wine. The temptation is hard to resist.

Part II

Effectiveness

and

Limitations

of

the

Scientific

Method

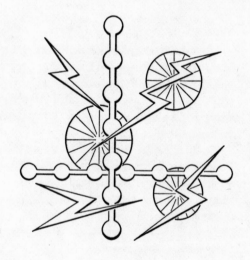

Chapter 4

Basic Research

BEFORE WE EXAMINE THE EFFECTIVENESS of the scientific method in solving the problems of man, let us first clarify its nature. The next five chapters are devoted to this undertaking. This particular chapter will dwell on the question of truth in science and its relation to the currently much touted emphasis on "basic research" as the path to truth and human welfare.

Science cannot float in a vacuum. She must have an anchorage. Philosophers have pondered for centuries over an eternal and universal point of reference. So far there have been deep probings and involved theorizings but no generally accepted conclusions. Meanwhile scientists relied on their senses. Perceptions became the foundations of their elaborations. What was sought was a coherent and concise arrangement of experience. Some workers have even staked out the extreme position that everything is unreal and empty in the universe save perceptions. But then perceptions in dreams would also be real. The Taoist Chuang-tze, who lived in the third century before Christ, put the dilemma thus: He once dreamt that he was a butterfly fluttering among the flowers of the spring forest. Suddenly he awoke. Was he a man who had dreamt that he was a butterfly or was he a butterfly who was then dreaming that he was a man?

Since facts do not lie, any discrepancy between data and concepts must be ascribed to defects in the concepts. So argues the theorist in his search for truth. He invites attention to the improvement of theoretical formulations.

Einstein envisions two components in scientific knowledge. One is immediately apprehended and empirically observed and the other is imagined or theoretically given. These two are joined by correlation. The single experiences are correlated with the theoretical structure. They are not tied together by logical relation or extensive abstraction. Thus the "blue" as observed color is correlated with the "blue" as wave length. The axiomatic basis of science must therefore be freely invented in Einstein's method of tentative deduction. As Northrop admirably points out, there are important implications to this way of thinking. It suggests that we cannot validly derive theoretical descriptions from empirical assertions. This would mean that knowledge gained from a priori theoretical constructs provides something different from experimental observations. Tentative deduction provides a knowledge of reality itself. This assumption enkindles the hope that truth itself can be approached through the scientific method.

Yet it is inconceivable that absolute truth will be given to mere man. Astronomers tell us that about twice the distance reached by the Mount Palomar telescope today represents the farthest we can ever hope to see. Beyond that point the galaxies of our expanding universe are receding from us at a rate faster than light. How can man, who boasts of only a few thousand years of literate knowledge in his million years of roaming this one speck of earth in one of a thousand million galaxies, each with a hundred billion stars, expect to peer into the secrets of the gods? And does man dare to extrapolate backward and forward infinite spans of space-time from his meager 400 years of scientific observations? Can his one mind encompass the interactions of infinite natures? Pilate was not merely posting a pretext when he asked, "What is truth?"

In contrast to Einstein most scientists have retreated from this barrage of questions. They have contented themselves with more tangible goals. Prevailing theories are modified in the light of more accurate observations. The feeling exists that successively refined measurements will lead to increasingly more precise predictions of events. Yet there is a limit to this progression. There are situations in mathematics, for example, in which the approximation to the solution becomes worse as computation is labored beyond a certain point. In experiments involving minute increments of matter, there is also a level of refinement beyond which a different set of rules comes into play. Bridgman makes the terse statement: "Events are not predictable in the realm of small things." Difficulties in the old Newtonian concepts were not dissolved by improvements along the same channel of thinking but by the introduction of radically new relativity concepts. We cannot extrapolate from thin statistical slices into the remote reaches of space and time.

Man has always been fond of fairy tales. Primitive men were strangers to the inanimate. Before the early days of the cipher and the alphabet animal forms were assigned to nature. The universe was composed of personalities. Babylonians used to say that the hot breath of the Bull of Heaven brought on the drought and scorched their crops until it was devoured by the giant bird Imdugud, which brought rain to the good people of Babylon. In modern times children find the stork and Santa Claus reassuring bearers of good tidings.

Until the mid-nineteenth century science had tried to purge herself of fictions. She had clung tenaciously to the search for the real world and clues to its unchanging principles. Twentieth century science, unable to divest herself of the human limitations in which her ideas were cast, began to follow the avenue of tentative concepts. She returned to the age of myths, although of a more convincing and useful order. Instead of the poetic and charming thoughts of Thor, humors and the like, there are now the id, free radicals, hyperon, and others.

Scientific figments have all been useful guides in their day of fashion. Consider, for example, the idea of force. It would have been extremely difficult for Newton to envision his first law of motion without the simplifying notion of one body exerting a tug-of-war control over the other. Force in this old and popular sense is no longer in vogue among the physicists. Instead of explaining that the sun exerts a force on the earth, the physicist now says that the earth is moving in the simplest fashion it possibly can in view of a particular "space-time relationship" to the sun.

Consider the concept of energy. What happens when a stone falls? It becomes a trifle warmer upon contact with the ground. So does the dirt around it. Where does the heat originate? From potential energy, the physicist used to say. Then what is potential energy? That energy the stone had before it fell, we were told. To lend reality to the circuit, decades of labor had been devoted to finding the substance of potential energy. Actually potential energy is merely a means of explaining the otherwise apparent discrepancies in another theory, that of the conservation of energy. This is not an unusual practice. We note that some of today's nuclear particles had been originally postulated for the purpose of balancing the mass-energy ledger in nuclear transformations. Nowadays, potential energy is no longer treated as a separate entity, and the law of conservation of energy itself is being modified.

Thoughts concerning space and time also have varied greatly over the years. Plato considered them as part of the World of Ideas. Spinoza ascribed space as an attribute of God. Kant felt that space and time are not distinct entities but actually represent our way of clothing sense perceptions as a means of imparting order to experience. Einstein subscribed to none of these, offering in their stead a relational system.

The relativity theory points out that many statements that were formerly thought susceptible of demonstrable truth are only definitions. They are just different ways of saying the same thing, such as the equivalence of a mile and 5280 feet. Croce stresses the proposition thus: "Science itself is nothing but a set of definitions, unified in a supreme definition; a system of concepts, or highest concept."

Ingenious theoretical superstructures live in constant dread of factual termites that continually gnaw at their foundations. They topple at the first inconsistency with observation. Concepts glory only in a relatively short term of office. We have witnessed the kaleidoscopic changes from Genesis to Darwin, from Ptolemy to Copernicus, from Boyle to van der Waals, from Newton to Einstein. This does not necessarily mean that no statements can be made about reality. It just means that science herself deals in temporary hypotheses of perfection at any given moment.

We have even observed, though only on rare occasions, how science has been hoodwinked by artifacts. This is illustrated by the rude awakening in 1953 that the Piltdown man was not real. At the time of his debut in 1908 he was given the dignified name *Eoanthropus dawsoni.* With the strange combination of a humanlike skull and an apelike jaw he appeared to be a natural missing link for the disciples of Darwin. The theory of evolution was finally being nailed firm. Unfortunately this was too good to last. Recently it was shown that a clever trickster had fitted an ape's jaw to a human cranium. With a bit of chemical aging and appropriate scientific releases, he had convinced the majority of the scientific world. It took science forty-five years to realize her gullibility.

So far, we have restricted ourselves to what the Buddhists call "truth in the common sense." If we are to examine "truth in the higher sense," the picture becomes far more complex, such as is being hinted at in scientific theories concerning universes of higher dimensions. It may be of some diversionary interest to glance at these "truths in the higher sense," in order to gain a broader perspective of the place of science in the world of thought. Chi-tsang, a great master of the Buddhist School of the Middle Path of the sixth century, delineated three levels of double truth. According to Fung Yu-lan's translation, these are:

> The common people take all things as really *Yu* (having being, existent) and know nothing about *Wu* (having no being, non-existent). Therefore the Buddhas have told them that actually all things are *Wu* and empty. On this level, to say that all things are *Yu* is the common sense truth and to say that all things are *Wu* is the higher sense truth.
>
> To say that all things are *Yu* is one-sided; but to say that all things are *Wu* is also one-sided. They are both one-sided, because they give people the wrong impression that *Wu* or non-existence only results from the absence of *Yu* or existence. Yet in actual fact, what is *Yu* is simultaneously what is *Wu*. For instance, the table standing before us need not be destroyed in order to show that it is ceasing to exist. In actual fact, it is ceasing to exist all the time. The reason for that is that when one starts to destroy the table, the table which one thus intends to destroy has already ceased to exist. The table of this actual moment is no longer the table of the preceding moment. It only *looks* like that of the preceding moment. Therefore on the second level of double truth, to say that all things are *Yu* and to say that all things are *Wu* are both equally common sense truth. What one ought to say is that the "not-one-sided middle path" consists in understanding that things are neither *Yu* nor *Wu*. This is the higher sense truth.
>
> But to say that the middle truth consists in what is not one-sided (i.e. what is neither *Yu* nor *Wu*), means to make distinctions. And all distinctions are themselves one-sided. Therefore on the third level, to say that things are neither *Yu* nor *Wu* and that herein lies the not-one-sided middle path, is merely common sense truth. The higher truth consists in saying that things are neither *Yu* nor *Wu*, neither not-*Yu* nor not-*Wu* and that the middle path is neither one-sided nor not one-sided.

So much for truth in the higher Buddhist sense, except to voice the opinion parenthetically that the silent feeling for such "higher truths" would appear necessary for sympathetic human understanding and effective international statesmanship. Let us return to the first level of common sense truth.

From this survey it can be seen that the world of science is fitted to our sense impressions through the development of concepts. These concepts are important maps to guide our thoughts and actions. It is recognized that a map is but a symbol and not in itself the earth and the river, the mountain and the plain. Nevertheless many concepts have been verified operationally. We feel safe in that if used within the purpose intended they can be treated as if they were true.

For practical purposes it does not really matter whether the general adaptation syndrome, the Newtonian law of gravitation, Laplace's nebular hypothesis, and the flatness of the earth are real or not. It is only important that the principles be useful. The scientific version of truth is based on the workability of the theory in practice and its ability to predict accurately within the limits of interest. According to this view, truth exists in the process by which the theory is confirmed. This is in distinct contrast to truth in the absolute sense, which antedates its own verification. In some respects the pragmatic approach provides science with a forward momentum. The theory must make contact with its empirical demonstration, which is yet to come. Unlike absolute truth, it does not look toward the antecedent. It generates an insatiable yearning for the next chapter in the action serial of life.

The assessment of utility is not an easy task. To a large extent the outcome depends upon the definitional system and the relational objective. A theory may be useful for a given purpose. It may not be for another. Hypotheses are therefore threatened with not only short lives but also narrow scopes. To be sure, the closer a concept approximates the unattainable reality, the greater will be its usefulness. For maximum value in use the theory should show agreement with empirical facts, definitiveness of claims, and simplicity of premises. The more extensive the area of effective application and the more natural or common sense the appearance, the more readily will the theory be accepted.

James' pragmatic rule locates the meaning of a statement in the concrete difference it makes in the course of human experience. If an alternative statement results in no sensible refractions it is considered the same notion but only known under another name. Questions concerning proposed differences between them are regarded as phantom problems.

This approach fits well the hands of science in her drive to change the world. She has upheld whatever tools are effective in use and discarded those that are ineffective. Assertability and not truth per se has become the focus of attention in the development of theories.

What seems to matter is that if we start with a given set of raw data we end up with another, which corresponds to our predictions. Since a welter of ad hoc hypotheses can satisfy this condition, there must be some guideline for the selection of the most acceptable one. Toward this end scientists feel that Occam's advice is good: "Entities are not to be complicated beyond necessity." The largest amount of voting facts are to be brought within the framework of a minimum set of axioms. Yet simplicity itself is not a simple affair. A theory may appear simple in the mathematical formulation describing the order and coherence of a world structure. Such are the final equations of Einstein. Yet it is not an easy exercise for man to picture or sense the curvature of space-time.

Careful analysis must be made before concluding that one theory is preferable to another. What is usually referred to as "descriptive simplicity" should not form a basis of choice. This type is illustrated by the greater ease of handling measures in the Continental over the British system. The pertinent variety is "inductive simplicity." This involves nonequivalent descriptions operating within the framework of inductive considerations. For example, the simplest curve through a mass of points on a graph is considered preferable to the infinite number of others that may be drawn.

Simplicity should not be mistaken for imaginative parsimony. Scientists should not confound the intent of Occam's Razor with a restricted insight into the infinite charm and variety of life. It is this confusion that misleads uninspired scientists to feel that nature has only a few facets and like a miser shows off only one at a time.

Let us recapitulate. Despite its aspirations for truth, science is not organized around it. It is organized around concepts. Its approach is not necessarily the path to reality but necessarily the path to utility. The utility of the concept lies in its verification. Industrialists invest money in the repeated verification of the concept of the electron. Farmers pledge generations of descendants to the same land in the repeated verification of the concept of the gene. Following such a dissection of the anatomy of the scientific effort, research can be broadly divided into two orientations: the development of concepts and the verification of concepts, and the unity of science lies in their fusion.

By and large scientists polarize toward one of the two attitudes. Those who seek new concepts are in the minority. By far the majority busy themselves with the verification of concepts. The latter includes the industrial scientists, engineers, and technologists, as well as many academicians who call themselves "basic researchers."

The currently muddled distinctions between "basic research" and "applied research" have long outlived their usefulness. There is much in common from the conceptual point of reference between the repeated confirmation of the Mendelian laws using the Black Angus cattle and that using the *Drosophila* fruit fly. The fact that a new strain of cattle may benefit the farmer but a new strain of fruit fly benefits no one does not make the former research "applied" and the latter "basic." To say that a given piece of research is "basic" because there is no foreseeable practical value attached to its completion may only be a myopic assessment of its usefulness. A keen and imaginative observer may well envision the highly utilitarian ramifications of the same work.

This discussion recalls to mind Hobbes' statement that "will is the last appetite in deliberation" and Dewey's dissertation on means and ends. According to Dewey's thesis, the end is merely an action viewed at a remote stage, whereas the means is part of the same series but viewed at an earlier stage. Means are merely the steps before the last in a proposed course of action. He therefore considers the terms to have no difference in reality but only in judgment. An analogy may be employed to distinguish between the so-called basic and so-called applied research. The precise nature of the momentary activity itself does not determine whether it is one or the other. It is to be considered "basic" if the scientist is oriented toward the development of new concepts. It is to be considered "applied" if he is oriented toward the verification, extension, or adaptation of prevailing concepts.

The formulation of concepts should be given much greater attention than it is receiving today. Even industry is recognizing its leavening importance on the vigor of the scientific society. Industry has generously supported free and independent researchers within the compass of its profit motives. Nobel laureate I. Langmuir at General Electric, W. Carothers at du Pont, and Nobel laureate C. J. Davisson at Bell Laboratories are notable examples of industry's appreciation of its significance. But we should hardly expect the business world to provide more than a stimulating amount of conceptual formulation in selected areas for its own purposes. The undirected development of concepts for the sheer enrichment of human thought is the traditional precinct of the ivy halls of learning. The academicians should note their privilege clearly and accept the attendant responsibilities in earnest. [Individual investigators in universities should not be beguiled by the financial lures of programs involving repeated conceptual applications.] In place of reduplicating and exaggerating current concepts, they should seek something new to say. [They should not attempt to compete with the efficiently organized industrial research teams in the area of semiroutine procedures worn smooth from repeated verifications.] Their forte is not in this arena but in the formulation of new theories, wherein realization is not a function of the massiveness of the apparatus, the magnitude of the budget, or the number of hands. The important things here are a passion for the ultimate, a humane sense of life, perspicacity of thought, and sincerity of purpose. An original concept, like Minerva, springs from one mind. It prefers the mind imbued with the love of Nature untainted with hidden plans for Her exploitation.

Chapter 5

Uncertainty of Scientific Knowledge

LET US CONTINUE THE ANALYSIS begun in the previous chapter on the nature of the scientific method. On how firm a foundation does it rest?

The abundance of accumulated data raises many questions concerning the origin of scientific knowledge. So far the answers hardly bear any semblance of unanimity. There is the attitude of Eddington who claims that many laws of science are epistemological. There is the skepticism of Santayana who alludes to the medley of presuppositions that greet our every experience. There is the view of Milne who prefers authoritarian principles as a basis for development. Flexible philosophical interpretations susceptible to being argued either way are also being advanced. The assortment brings to mind the versatile Teng Shih who lived a generation before Confucius. The story about him goes as follows: The body of a wealthy man was recovered from the Wei River by a fisherman who asked for a rather large sum of money from the family. The family asked Teng for advice. "Hold on," suggested Teng, "no other family will pay for the body." Thereupon the family waited. As time went on, the fisherman became anxious and he too came to Teng for counsel. "Hold on," said Teng, "from nobody else can they obtain the body."

The notion of cause and effect is the touchstone of the scientific method. [Fundamentally scientists are causationists.] They do not want to believe that things go along higgledy-piggledy, unrestrained by the tension of an invariable succession of effect after cause. [Where the cause is unknown scientists find it more acceptable to believe that there are causes beyond their grasp than to admit that there are no causes at all.] It is here that we must direct first attention if we are to determine the degree of confidence with which we should give to our scientific conclusions. In other words, just how certain is the research premise of cause and effect?

In this regard a distinction should be made between the terms "explanation" and "causality." A cause is a relation between phenomena. One event gives rise to the next; applying a certain factor brings out other definite changes; prolonging a given situation continues another. Explanation, on the other hand, is simply information that bears on a puzzling event and makes it less puzzling. An explanation may be causal, but [any notion, faith, or fact that relieves a person's perplexity and enables him to account for real or apparent discrepancies among his observations] is an explanation.

The Hindus disposed of the question of cause and effect quite simply. They abolished it. According to them cause and effect are actually the same thing observed from different vantage points. The effect is latent in the cause. The Vedanta explains that only when a cause exists is an effect observed. Their conjoint nature can be noticed in an aggregate of threads, for example, which gives rise to a fabric. Instead of perceiving what we call cloth, we observe only threads along the warp and the filling. Within the threads are still finer threads, then finer fibers, and so on. On this basis we can say that the ultimately finest parts constitute the cause.

Sometimes the existence of the cause cannot be observed in the effect. This is exemplified by the acorn from which springs the great oak. The term birth is applied to the process by which the causal substance in the seed becomes visible in the tree. Death is the reversal of the process. In this case the cause passes beyond the sphere of visibility. This doctrine of Sat-kâryavâda states that every effect pre-exists. We can draw on the simile of the rope mistaken for a snake. There is the very real effect of frightening those who step upon it.

A modern analogy to the Hindu's fusion of cause and effect is given by the mathematical economist, Vilfredo Pareto. The independent variable in an algebraic equation is frequently considered the cause. Pareto pointed out that this may not be a generally admissible translation. A commonly accepted characteristic of cause is that it necessarily precedes the effect. The market price of an article may be considered an effect of the cost of production, which is the cause. The thought may be turned around so that the cost of production becomes the effect of the sales price, which is then regarded as the cause. The mutual dependence between supply and demand can be interpreted in either direction. The supply of the product on the market may precede the demand or vice versa. In describing such mutually dependent terms we can only say that there is an equation relating them. Pareto concluded that we must restrict the colloquial description of cause and effect to special cases and these only with considerable circumspection.

The propensity of scientists toward analysis and isolating as many factors as possible is quite a departure from the organic views of the Hindus. Scientists prefer to treat cause and effect as separate entities and to focus attention on their relation. The first modern and also the most devastating philosophical treatment of causation was advanced by Hume about two hundred years ago. He concluded that knowledge involving causal relation is uncertain and at best only probable. Such a skeptical analysis is difficult for science to accept. But as the subsequent paragraphs will show, it is also difficult to refute.

Hume begins with the premise that all our reasoning concerning matters of fact is based on the postulated relation of cause and effect. Only through causation can one event be inferred from another. It is therefore important to know on what grounds our conclusions regarding this relation rest.

Descartes and the Scholastics had previously considered cause and effect as necessary connections. This assumes the presupposition "*A* causes *B*." Hume proceeded to show that sense experience is what provides knowledge of cause and effect. The knowledge is not one of logical or intuitive certainty. Experience in *A* alone does not lead to *B*. The requisite experience must involve the constant sequential conjunction of *A* with *B*. According to Hume, the statement "*A* causes *B*" means only that *A* and *B* are found conjoined. The reason for the connection remains in the dark. After we have repeatedly seen the same sequence of one event following another, the next time we are confronted with an impression of the first, we also conjure up an idea of the second. In other words, the percept of *A* is connected with the idea of *B*. *A* as an object is not connected with *B* as an object.

Hume concludes that objects have no discoverable cause and effect connection between them. Causation is not an independent relation but merely a sequential derivation. He argues further that experience of frequent conjunction in the past does not necessarily guarantee the same conjunction in the future. The supposition that the future resembles the past is derived entirely from custom.

Marcus Long's story of the chicken with scientific proclivities illustrates Hume's thinking rather delightfully:

> A little chicken sitting comfortably in the henhouse without a care in the world was startled by the appearance of a man and ran away. When it came back the man was gone but there was some corn lying on the ground. Having a degree of scientific curiosity the chicken began to watch and it soon noticed that when the man appeared the corn appeared. It did not want to commit itself to any theory in a hurry and watched the sequence 999 times. There were no exceptions to the rule that the appearance of the man meant food, so it swallowed its skepticism and decided there must be a necessary connection between the man and the corn. In the language of causality this meant that whenever the man appeared the corn *must* appear. On the basis of this conclusion it went out to meet the man on his thousandth appearance to thank him for his kindness and *had its neck wrung*.

As far as the physical sciences are concerned Russell agrees wholly with Hume. The simple rules of the form "*A* causes *B*" are usually admitted in the early stages of experimental planning as crude points of departure, so Russell points out. As refinements evolve, these simple statements are gradually replaced by pictures so complex that they extend beyond the limits of perception. They then become elaborate inferences.

Whitehead, however, insists that if we are to solve the difficulty which stopped Hume we must search not in the accumulation of instances but in the intrinsic character of each instance which would justify the belief. It must be known by relatedness, since spatiotemporal relation is a necessary presupposition of Hume's philosophy. The key is what Whitehead calls "an instance of the ingression of sense-objects amid events" and the passage of this ingression of sense-objects to the perceptual objects, such as dogs, horses, and trees. Both terms have the pervasive property through time. Unlike the other, the sense-object is derived "from its ingression in nature, which is an irreducible many-termed relation." Unfortunately, as Whitehead admits, this relation is not easy to clarify. To pursue it further through the control of ingression by Aristotelian pervasive adjectives is beyond the intended scope of this book as well as the competence of its author. Nevertheless, we must recognize the severe blow that Hume struck at the very root of the scientific method. Until Hume is successfully refuted, the current scientific approach can only be regarded as a workable expedient, far removed from logical infallibility. The famous physicist Planck proposed a compromise: "Causality is neither true nor false. It is a most valuable heuristic principle to guide science in the direction of promising returns in an ever progressive development."

Hume's blow to the certainty of the scientific method was followed by another. It was the statistical conclusion of Bolzmann and Gibbs. In the Newtonian days of the eighteenth and nineteenth centuries the same set of laws was applied to all kinds of systems. It did not matter to the physicist that the systems were characterized by different positions and momenta. They all were supposed to obey the same laws which are considered rigid and unchangeable. What Bolzmann and Gibbs did a century ago was to show that this is not so. Even systems with the same amount of energy are not described forever by fixed patterns. There is a tenuous hedge of contingency. Nature's secrets are matters of probability.

Attempts have been made to reconcile the principle of probability in science with the causation concept. The argument was advanced that discrepancies arise simply from our inability to measure to the necessary degree of refinement. Probability is considered merely a temporary haze of ignorance. However, Bridgman emphasizes that the essential point is not interference with the situation by the act of observation but interference to an unpredictable and incalculable amount. This unpredictability is due to nature herself and not to our inability to make precise measurements. Modern statistical theory began separating different sources of error. In atomic physics, for example, the "uncontrolled errors" are distinguished from the "errors due to technique." Heisenberg's Uncertainty Relations reinforced this feeling of probability in scientific measurements.

Meanwhile science is becoming increasingly aware of the interconnectedness of events in the universe. She is doubting the old atomic idea of separate entities, cleanly severable from each other. Events are being considered as inextricable features of a totality. Accordingly, causality may be viewed as the system under certain conditions which bring emphasis upon a single facet of its myriad components. According to this point of view, cause, when it implies a single factor, is meaningless. If you add sodium to water is sodium the cause of the liberation of hydrogen? Or is water? Or both? Can there be gaseous liberation without time? Or space? Conversely, can time flow without substance? Can space expand without content?

We gather from this sketchy outline that the causation cornerstone of rational knowledge is somewhat shaky. It may be instructive at this point to look at a few philosophical schools most relevant to the scientific attitude and see how their treatments of the source of knowledge agree with our actual experience in life. The three selected are critical idealism, positivism, and critical realism.

As we have seen from the previous discussion, Hume's consistent extension of empiricism led to a conclusion most unpalatable to science. It shook the very foundation of scientific induction. It is not surprising that violent antagonisms arose against Hume's doctrine. The most influential of these was Kant's Transcendental or Critical Idealism. Kant could not bring himself to feel that science with all her progress was just a matter of custom. There must be something which ties events together in an ordered fashion. Causality is considered one of these principles of order used by the mind. Let us see how Kant developed his thesis.

Kant recognized that the individualistic conception of experience cannot meet Hume's attack upon the notion of causality. He also saw that to obtain cognition the individual must join together the separate segments of his observations and experience. Extension of Hume's analysis showed that this connection is not a quality of the given material as such, and other philosophers had convinced Kant that neither is it found in the formal products of thinking. This led Kant to the core of the dilemma. It is the analysis of experience to find out how the bits and pieces are related to form cognition on the part of the observer.

In approaching the problem Kant distinguished between two pairs

The Tao of Science

of propositions. The first pair involves "analytic" and "synthetic" propositions. An analytic one contains the predicate as part of the subject. "A successful industrialist is an industrialist" is an example. The truth of such an assertion follows naturally. To maintain that a successful industrialist is not an industrialist would be self-contradictory. The truth of synthetic propositions, on the other hand, cannot be gained merely from an analysis of the statement. Propositions dependent on experience belong to this class. "Stevens is an imaginative executive" is an example.

The other pair involves "empirical" and "a priori" propositions. Empirical propositions depend on observations and sense perceptions; scientific laws fall into this group. A priori ones do not arise from experience, even though they may be elicited by it. They are necessary for guiding human thinking. Pure mathematics belongs in this class.

Hume had claimed that science increases our knowledge only through experience. This would mean that science is empirical and synthetic. No certainty can accordingly be expected in scientific predictions. Kant, however, feels that science does increase our knowledge and at the same time makes predictions with certainty. In other words synthetic judgments a priori should be possible.

In order to develop his thesis Kant advanced the forms of intuition or "categories" of: quantity (unity, plurality, totality), quality (reality, negation, limitation), relation (substance-and-accident, cause-and-effect, reciprocity), and modality (possibility, existence, necessity). According to Kant things are unknowable in themselves. They only cause sensations in us. These sensations are ordered in our mental apparatus by means of these categories, space, and time. The categories serve as subjective spectacles, with which we mentally look at the outside world. It is only through the ordering of sense perceptions through these categories that we arrive at the concepts by means of which we understand experience.

Russell examined Kant's categories and found them far from convincing. Kant's theory of space and time does not explain why we see things arranged as they seem to be and not otherwise. Why is the nose always seen above the mouth and not vice versa? The nose and the mouth may be considered as things in themselves. They may elicit individual sensations in our minds. Yet there is no place in the discussion to account for the sensation of spatial arrangement. The difficulty is accentuated in the case of time. Why is it that we always see the lightning before we hear the thunder?

Kant's argument that geometry is a priori although synthetic is likewise faulty. Russell explains that geometry is of two types. One type is illustrated by pure geometry, which belongs to the logical variety. It is not synthetic. The other type, such as the general theory of relativity, is a branch of physics which is an empirical science in which the axioms are inferred from observations. The first is a priori and not synthetic and the second is synthetic and not a priori.

There are other weaknesses in Kant's thesis. These have been brought out particularly by Einstein's theory of relativity. Without going into details, the relativity implications strongly suggest that knowledge within the Kantian frames of thought is not possible. Einstein's physics thus became one of the important forces behind the recent trend toward empiricism. Empiricism covers such a number of variants that it is not feasible to attempt to describe all of them in this survey. One of the forms of empiricism more fashionable among scientists is modern positivism, which we shall briefly cover.

Although modern positivism subscribes to Kant's assertion that a priori knowledge of the independent real world is impossible, it does not believe in the concept of categories. It claims that facts should be the sole corpus of human knowledge. These facts are simple descriptions of sensory phenomena. Positivism discourages metaphysical speculations and introspective psychology. Statements that cannot be directly or indirectly established by experience cannot be considered as describing something real. "God is the creator of heaven and earth" is an example. No one can test the truth of this statement because there is no appeal to supporting or negating experience. The situation is quite different with the statement that "Gardner weighs 224 pounds," for the direct verification of which we need only point to the scale.

Against this background of positivism Bridgman advances a pragmatic operational analysis of physical concepts. He reasons that in order to understand a term, the conditions of use must be made clear. Otherwise the idea cannot be substantiated. The meaning of a concept is therefore obtained from an analysis of its operations in actual cases. Terms that cannot be reduced to operations are considered meaningless. The term "absolute length," for example, is regarded as purely verbal because there is no procedure by which it can be exhibited. The concept of infinity falls into the same class. When it is defined in terms of impossible manipulations, paradoxes are certain to arise. But when infinity is defined in terms of feasible operations, it can be handled quite legitimately.

Unfortunately operational analysis is not as simple as it sounds at first voicing. In sociology and other less precise disciplines it assumes more of a verbal nature. Processes involving the past are also principally rhetorical and require cautious handling. For example, it would be difficult to reduce the following statement to verifying operations: "The universe was created two minutes ago in just the condition we think it as a result of two billion years of evolution." Nor is the famous question of W. K. Clifford any easier: "May not the entire universe be uniformly contracting in dimensions, everything together, our standards of length as well as everything else?"

Furthermore, the conditions under which the operations are to be executed must be stated precisely. Operations implemented at one order of magnitude may not provide the same outcome when repeated at another. The length of a moving automobile is the same whether it is measured by laying a yardstick alongside it during movement or by taking an instantaneous photograph, which is subsequently measured. However, an identical answer would not be obtained by the two methods were the car travelling at the speed of light.

The critical realists agree with many schools of philosophy on the existence of an objective world independent of one's mind. In this sense they differ from the idealists. Although they believe in the possibility of knowledge, they also recognize the difficulties involved in affirming this realism. There are many shades of critical realists, but they all refuse to admit that the only alternative to subjective idealism is the other extreme of naïve realism. They argue against simple or absolute objectivisms. According to these realists knowledge concerns external objects. These external objects are responsible for the ideas we have. Ideas are immediately known, whereas objects are inferred from the ideas generated. The mediating ideas are therefore different from the inferred things.

Santayana, a poetic critical realist, went into considerable detail regarding the way knowledge is obtained. He asserts that there is mind and there is substance. By means of intuition the mind perceives essence; by means of awareness it knows substance. Thus knowledge consists of two jumps: one of intuition from the mind to some essence and the other of faith and of action from a symbol in the mind to the outside object. The intuitive essences, which exist in physical objects, are supposed to awaken an awareness in us. As constituents of nature these physical objects are independent of the mind and are unknowable. However, Santayana does not explain satisfactorily how the mind evolves and how it intuits essence. What the mechanism is in obtaining knowledge of an object remains unclear. How can we be sure that the world which we immediately know resembles the world which we mediately know? How can we see a test tube in its unseen state? It appears that critical realism is caught on the horns of a dilemma. If it pursues the inaccessibility of the objective world it ends in skepticism. It will be unable to prove even the existence of the objective world. But if it stresses the similarity of the objective and the mental world, it ends in idealism, which it had set out to displace.

In summary, we appear at a loss trying to grasp the origin and nature of knowledge. It seems that the more rigorously we attempt to establish the basis for scientific knowledge, the more confused we become. Dejectedly, we read the account of the invitation of the Rockefeller Foundation to the American Philosophical Society after World War II to "undertake an examination of the present state of philosophy and the role philosophy might play in the postwar world." In creditable frankness, the Committee of the Society states in the Introduction of the Report: "There is not in our contemporary situation an authoritatively accepted body of doctrine called 'philosophy' for which duly accredited spokesmen can pretend to speak. There are philosophies and philosophers, and they differ philosophically on just the issues with which we are called upon to deal."

Early man, too, seems to have been confounded by similar contradictions and uncertainties. His unscientific mind came to his succor in strange ways. It was not unusual for the ancients to admit the simultaneous validity of several rationally incompatible approaches. The multiforms of the gods are an example. Babylonians had worshipped the generative force in nature as a lion-headed bird in rain, as a snake in soil fertility, and as a man in the statues of their temples. In ancient

Egypt, conviction in the inclusiveness of nature was expressed by tolerantly accepting some of the logically most divergent paradoxes interwoven into a single fabric of belief. Among the Hindus we find the creative force, Kali, in her transient conflicting forms. At one moment she is a beautiful young girl; at another she is a terrible ogress. She shows up at times with her long tongue licking up the world, as it were, with threatening fangs, but a slender, full-breasted body. At the same time she both cherishes and devours her children.

Far from being irrational mumbo jumbo these practices have deep philosophical significance. The varying guises and multifaceted appearances of the gods are pregnant poetic expressions of the complexity of nature. The ancients had anticipated Hume and answered him in their own mystical fashion. Their message to adolescent science struggling with Hume's challenge seems to be: Sometimes the less rational way is the more reasonable solution.

Chapter 6

Logic, Fallacy, Paradox, Common Sense

NO PHRASE FLASHES ACROSS THE MIND of the executive more often than: Is it logical? He prides himself on his powers of logic. The more "scientific" he is, the more he tries to shape his decisions by stern logic. Let us therefore scout its main features and see how they shade into common sense in the texture of experience.

Logical thought is classified into two kinds: inductive and deductive. Inductive logic divines the general law governing the behavior of events from a given set of observations. Deductive logic infers special events in accordance with assumed laws.

In the process of induction, science attempts to relate subordinate inductions into more comprehensive ones. The latter are tested by observations in properly designed experiments. Upon repeated confirmation the general laws are accepted as valid by simple enumeration. Accordingly, Bacon believed that if skill and care are exercised in the orderly arrangement of cases, the universal governing law would make itself obvious through an almost mechanical process.

Keynes has advanced a subtle analysis of the difficulties underlying induction. He agrees that the reliability of the conclusions improves with repetition. Previous workers had assumed the reason to be a straightforward matter of random probabilities based on a uniformity of nature. Not so, says Keynes. The higher degree of assurance is due to the increased confidence that the recurring studies cover only the pertinent characteristics in common. Consequently it is reasonable to expect diminishing chances of an unsuspected factor upsetting the applecart in the succeeding attempt. For such sequences, however, the premise must permit the assumption that the relevant factors belong to a finite system. Otherwise inductive arguments would not provide even probable knowledge.

From the penumbra of deliberations on induction sprang many philosophic explanations. Whewell stresses the dependence of induction on the correct premise. Mach feels that natural laws are merely short-hand representations of perceptions. Feigl considers induction an operational rule. Reichenbach uses it as an instrument to predict future events in the fashion of a wager. Wittgenstein grounds the laws of induction on a psychological instead of a logical base as the simplest to account for our experience. Finally Whitehead argues that since induction rests upon an antecedent rationalism, it actually presupposes metaphysics. To have a rational justification for past events, metaphysics must assure us that there *is* a past. To have a rational justification for future predictions, metaphysics must assure us that there *is* an already determined future. Induction therefore is not the derivation of general laws but the prophecy of some characteristics of a particular future from the known characteristics of a particular past.

In the corroboration of theories or in questions of prediction, the matter of inductive probability is involved. The gambler's odds of five to ten are different from the economic statistician's of five to ten. The latter are a likelihood of frequency. It means that five out of every ten persons are working under the circumstances under discussion. The gambler's quotation is a case of inductive probability. In order to earn five dollars in a wager, we will have to risk ten. [Inductive probability depends more on the evidence in the possession of the observer than on a property of the object under consideration.] It does not predict frequency; it merely evaluates evidence based on logical analysis. In the planning of experiments for testing hypotheses, the scientist emulates the art of the gambler rather than that of the economist.

In the dissection of scientific problems there is a tendency to assume that one law out of a given set of alternatives can be selected through induction. This practice is useful especially in the early stages of experimentation. Research requires the adoption of some hypothesis as a necessary step to organizing data. Otherwise there is no way of judging relevance. Without the concepts of matter, molecule, energy, space, time, and number, the enumeration of facts would be largely haphazard. As one proceeds in the refinement of concepts and experimental plans, the constancy of the initial guide becomes progressively doubtful. Formerly is was felt that laws do not alter the fundamental notions from which they grew. Today it is recognized that the very process of determination of the laws may change the underlying principles. The framing of concepts is still the misty and difficult aspect of scientific work. Despite the centuries of experience in their formulation, a rule prescribing the invention of new ones is still wanting.

In the deductive process a set of assumptions is made by means of which new theorems are elicited. Accepting the suppositions, one also must grant the theorems. To go no further than this short step would not provide deduction with much value. From such a limited perspective many researchers have accepted Bacon's view that deductive reasoning provides nothing original. Since the results are already contained in the premises, deduction was considered to be of limited use. Actually this is an oversimplified devaluation. The part played in science by deduction is much greater than Bacon cared to concede. In order to test the validity of a theory, some predicted event must first be set, which is to be checked by subsequent observation. To derive the logical consequence from the stated postulate is at times a long process involving premise, deduction, and conclusion. Furthermore, knowing the premise does not necessarily mean that we concurrently apprehend the conclusion. We need to carry out sequential analysis involving mathematical logic and other deductive tools. They enable us to deal with abstract ideas and conjure up new hypotheses, which may otherwise be overlooked.

Logic is thus an organizing lattice for the natural sciences. It examines the derivation of concepts from observed facts. It analyzes the structure of the general propositions put forward and determines their interrelationships. It deduces the phenomena expected under various conditions.

We must however guard against the glib use of logic. It is endangered by foggy passages and hidden pitfalls. Let us take the exemplary case of mathematics. It is recognized as the acme of certitude among the sciences. A simple illustration is the multiplication table. Thrice seven is twenty-one. This is positively certain. Yet if we advance just one more step and ask, "Just what are these cardinal numbers?", we become quite puzzled. We talk about seven water buffaloes and twenty-one abacuses. But just what are seven and twenty-one apart from the items? Then there are the ordinal numbers: the seventh water buffalo and the twenty-first abacus. How are seven and seventh related? In what way is the "half" in half-a-pound similar to the "half" in half-a-foot? *Is* there such a thing as half of a man, or half of a family? A similar lack of explicit clarity exists in the interpretation of other basic mathematical notions, such as points, lines, and planes.

Most loose reasoning arises from extralogical considerations. If we say, "Since some doctors are cardiologists, all doctors must be," we commit a logical mistake. But if we say, "Mario is right, right is opposed to left, therefore Mario is opposed to left," we are in error extralogically. The syllogism would have been valid had the term "right" meant the same thing in both premises, but the illustrated sequence is fallacious, because "right" did not. Seneca's example of this common class of erroneous arguments goes along as follows: "Mouse is a syllable; mouse eats cheese; therefore some syllables eat cheese." This is an incorrect application of the valid syllogism: "If all b is a and all b is c, then some c is a."

Begging the question is another flaw. "I am promoting Jo because she is competent," we may hear an executive say. But when he is asked how he knows Jo to be competent he replies, "Because I am going to promote her!" This is a misapplication of the law of tautology which says: "If propositions a, b, c, . . . are all true then a is true." He had assumed the proposition which is to be proven.

Appeal to authority is a common refuge of the intellectual sloth. Introductory phrases like "Aristotle says . . ." and "The Prime Minister says . . ." always provide an initial advantage to the speaker. The listener should not be inordinately swayed by such references.

The trap of many questions brings up the familiar "Have you stopped beating your wife?" It assumes that every question has a "yes" or "no" answer. This follows from the law of the excluded middle, which states that all propositions are either true or false.

Argument from analogy is not usually considered fallacious because of its usefulness, but it is a dangerous tool and the derived conclusions are never rigorous. Analogy is not identity and considerable restraint must be exercised in its employment.

The false cause or non sequitur fallacy has been committed repeatedly by Sherlock Holmes. In this group necessary premises are omitted.

The fallacy of accidents confuses the accidental with the essential.

Oversimplification or reductive fallacy is a frequent blunder in management. This occurs when one feature of the total is singled out and a judgment of the whole is pronounced on the basis of that single element. It is a source of much irritation in the compartmentalized bureaucracy of large institutions in which various offices are vested each with a stop-and-go light.

Related to the reductive fallacy is the confusion of categories. The chemist, the biologist, the physicist, the comptroller, the production manager, the admiral, the politician, the artist—each has his own tradition, language, medium, and values. The confusion of categories leads to the assumption that the rules of the game played by one group can be followed by the other. Each can be expected to continue where the other leaves off. The biologist should base his further research on what the physicist says of life. The artist should accept the moral conviction of the patron and give it an emotional color. The chemist should conduct fruitful research under operational directives laid down for production plants. The same managerial policies and practices should be equally applicable to the production of shirts, the invention of hardware, and the discovery of concepts. All management would thus be congealed in one mold.

Actually, each functional species may require a different treatment. One profession is not an edited copy of another. For an organization involving many disciplines and operational classes, only a broad, all-encompassing managerial code should be adopted, one which is capable of adjusting in turn to each of the individual elements. The degree of dispersion of the administration of authority should be determined by the latitude necessary to balance the optimal expression of the separate natures against the simultaneous diffusion of synthesis by top management.

Besides the many fallacies that have bothered logicians there are the equally annoying paradoxes. The most famous is the Epimenides paradox. Epimenides, a Cretan, was reported to have said: "All Cretans are liars." The question is: Are they?

Another riddle is Russell's: The librarian was asked to make a complete catalogue of just those books in the library which do not mention themselves in their contents. Should the catalogue which is to remain in the library, list itself?

A third is the dilemma paradox. This takes the form of a charming tale: A beautiful maiden fell out of her canoe into the hands of the conscientious king of the alligators. To be sporting about the mother's appeal for her daughter's return, the alligator king offered to free her if the mother could state one true proposition. Intuitively the lady said, "You are going to keep my daughter." Should the daughter be released?

Infinite regress is still another logical perplexity. This can be exemplified by the poor artist in a building, trying to draw an exact picture of everything in it. As he began to insert a drawing of his own drawing into the drawing, he had to include a smaller drawing of the entire version in his drawing of the drawing of the drawing, ad infinitum. When does he stop?

At this point, it may be well to look briefly into the relationship of logic to reality. Traditional empiricism teaches that logic must be validated through actual sense experience. Out of many empirical observations a generalization is derived. In effect logic and mathematics are considered the symbolic representation of the resulting fundamental laws. Since logic thus circumscribes the laws of nature it should be testable by experience. This implies a correction in our mathematical propositions each time they are contradicted. When we are short-changed at the grocers the multiplication table will have to be modified! While we would not hesitate to disbelieve the empirical findings rather than the a priori validity of the multiplication table in this simple situation, the decision is not as clean cut in the more involved cases.

For many years the disturbing problem remained: Should empiricism or the a priori validity of logic be abandoned? The Vienna Circle philosophers developed a reasonable explanation. The group felt that logic does not establish laws of the objective world. It makes no assertions about reality. It concerns itself only with logical relations, not factual ties. The logical connections are formulated without regard to concrete particulars. They are principles of combination and order within the limits of the symbolic system. Thus the relation $3 + 2 = 5$ is simply a grouping of two units into one within the rules of arithmetic. There is nothing articulate about real items in the equation. The entire manipulation occurs within a symbolic system which never changes. Consequently the validity of logic must be a priori. It is not refutable by empirical observations. According to this line of reasoning the Vienna School revised the teachings of some earlier empiricists who stated that all knowledge is dependent on experience. There is a dualism: the logical assertions independent of experience and the empirical assertions testable by experience. The two are not to be confused.

From this rambling outline we get an inkling of the shifty status of logic in our day-to-day activities. On the one hand, logic is considered rigorous and helpful, and on the other hand, it often leads to fallacies and paradoxes. It pretends to be the ultimate laws of reason, according to which the world is to be interpreted; yet some of the most astute personalities of history have never heard of syllogisms. Many philosophers regard logic as the long-awaited substitute for the ancient, eroded ontological metaphysics. Others consider logic mere rhetoric of the A is A variety.

The rules of logic require the mind for their proper formulation and application. Yet the mind itself rests more comfortably among the acquaintances of common sense. We hear E. M. Forster's Old Lady put it this way: "Logic! Good gracious! What rubbish! How can I tell what I think till I see what I say?" John Quincy Adams wrote in a different but related vein to Chief Justice John Marshall: "I told him it was law logic—an artificial system of reasoning, exclusively used in courts of justice, but good for nothing anywhere else." Justice Benjamin Cardozo is reported to have described the contradiction of legal inheritance to current trends thus: "A judge must think of himself as an artist, who although he must know the handbooks, should never trust to them for his guidance; in the end he must rely upon his almost instinctive sense of where the line lay between the word and the purpose which lay behind it; he must somehow be true to both."

Common sense alone tells us what to do after all logic has failed. Let us take a simple example: One and one are two. In the further study of this sentence we meet with ambiguous ramifications. Obviously one thing and itself make only one. So the sentence must be expanded to: One thing and another thing make two things. Yet one must be certain of the nature of things that are put together. One apple plus another apple is quite different from one apple plus one horse. Furthermore the environment under which things are put together casts a decided influence on the outcome. As Whitehead pleasantly notes, every hostess takes account of this truth in her invitations.

In practice, therefore, logic is not divorced from circumstances. Sometimes the background is especially relevant; sometimes it is not. Only common sense can tell us which holds and when. Nature does not respond to the forced purity of logic. The words of the great painter Cézanne are worth remembering in this respect: "There is a logic of colors, and it is with this alone, and not with the logic of the brain that the painter should conform."

In the application of logic to a particular situation we must keep several processes clear. We must make sure that there are no purely logical fallacies, particularly those of a sequential nature. In the urge to construct elaborate scientific hypotheses, it is very human to overlook some slight deviation from common sense, which ultimately may introduce a wide variance. We must ensure that the postulates hold for the concrete case under consideration. Logic does not give us the answer; it is left for other intuitions. We must be especially aware of the foundation, which is frequently the weakest point of the edifice. Something might have been presupposed which is not warranted. Unnecessary assumptions might have been added which might serve only to confuse the issue. As Giordano Bruno said, "If the first button of a man's coat is wrongly buttoned, all the rest will be crooked." The keenest logic and the most adept mathematical transformations cannot produce a tittle without a sound premise. Zero begets zero.

Therefore, knowledge of the valid types of logic and the concentration of mind to follow them are not sufficient to produce a good reasoner. The essence of the art lies in grasping the problem at the right end and getting to the core of the ideas around which relevant facts are marshaled. Logic becomes just one of the guides; it is not a commander. In formal logic contradiction is disastrous, but not necessarily in life. It may be an invitation to new fascinations. Discrepancy is the doorway to discovery.

Chapter 7

Why Quibble over Words?

THE EXECUTIVE MILIEU is thick with verbosity. Conferences, discussions, speeches, and reports follow each other in endless procession. The apt usage of words and symbols is of great importance in the art of executive life. This chapter attempts to delineate a healthy respect for the strength and limitations of words and symbols as a basis for proper manipulation.

In order to reason man must fabricate symbolic versions of his experience. A facility at symbol formation is one of his unique capabilities. Animals rely on the raw pictures of concrete circumstances. They cannot use signs to represent something in the abstract, to think about events in absentia. To them signs indicate merely something immediately forthcoming. Man, on the other hand, is surrounded by symbols —the cross, the striped pole before the barber shop, the three balls before the pawn shop, the red and green traffic lights, and the partisan cartoons in the newspapers. The ink marks at which you are looking represent words, which are themselves emblematic of ideas and things. There are the deeds, the musical scores, the maps, and the blueprints. There are the tokens of prestige: the M.D.'s, the Ph.D.'s, the mahogany panels and rugs in the president's office. Without man's ability to produce and respond to symbols, language would be sterile as a medium of communication. And without language and its informative quality, thought itself would be severely handicapped. Instead of defining man as an animal *rationale,* Cassirer accordingly calls him an animal *symbolicum.*

Because of our inheritance and physiology, vocal signs have been the most efficient in the development of symbolic thought and expression. But words are not the only forms of articulation. The symbolic world can be grasped by less effective means. The remarkable activities of Helen Keller have demonstrated this quite convincingly.

Wiener illustrated the transmission of ideas without words and sign language by his imaginary meeting in the woods with an intelligent savage. All Wiener had to do was to remain alert to those movements when the primitive fellow showed emotion or interest. He then fixed what he saw or heard in his own mind. Before long Wiener had discovered the things that were important to the native, not because of any communication from the man but because of observations by Wiener. The ability of the savage to pick out Wiener's own moments of special attention became in itself a sort of language almost as varied in scope as the impressions both of them could encompass. Accordingly, Wiener feels that social animals might have had active, intelligent, and variable means of communication long before the existence of language.

Many scientists insist that the highest purpose of human knowledge is to provide the facts and nothing but the facts. But just what is a scientific fact? The last three chapters have taken us through a murky search for the answer to this question. We emerged with the feeling that the facts of science imply a theoretical as well as an empirical element. The composing of theories and formulae is a symbol-making activity. The results are not ultimate insights but assuring symbols of nature. The scientific world thus becomes a sphere of man-made symbols, and scientists are the most prolific architects.

To a great degree scientists are like sculptors and painters. As Malraux has shown, regardless of whether he is a recluse like Gauguin and Cézanne or a missionary like Van Gogh or an exhibitor on the Rialto like young Tintoretto, the great painter transforms the meaning of the world which he masters, by converting it to a form he has developed. This form is usually derived from one that was handed down by an immediate predecessor. The researcher behaves in an analogous manner. He depicts the world in scientific laws and concepts.

Before we essay further on the nature of language, just what can be transmitted by it? What is detailed is a specification of a particular quality in relation to another. A blue color is stated as that color of Alice's blue dress. The qualitative content is described within a manifold and determined through its relationship. Ultimately what is designed by a word or a sentence is something to which one can point.

The same holds true for poetry as well as scientific propositions. Feeling and intuition are not relayed to the reader; they are evoked. The excitation is effective if the position of the qualitative within the designated order gives rise to the same images in the reader as in the writer. Whether or not two persons who perceive the same manifold also experience the same qualitative content cannot be ascertained. The only point a psychologist can clarify is whether or not they make the same assertions. He can only discover whether or not the qualities experienced by the two persons appear in the same relation to other qualities. By itself qualitative content is strictly an incommunicable, private affair. This is an important point to bear in mind when "iron-clad" laws, contracts, and treaties are being drafted. As Bernard Berenson states, "Representation is a compromise with chaos."

Language may be roughly divided into three kinds: descriptive, action, and poetic. The aim of descriptive language is to record or transfer accurate data and messages. It is used in scientific treatises, financial statements, and blueprints. Words are exchanged among individuals with intuitive acquaintance as well as systematic knowledge. They refer to things and events primarily outside of the subjective participants. Disagreements can be resolved by objective observations.

Action language does not stress exactness. Its purpose is to incite activity, to inhibit participation, or to arouse passions. Action language abounds in advertisements, rituals, commands, and sermons. Politicians are experts in its gab. A word delivered under one set of circumstances may be descriptive. The same word under different auspices, with a varying intonation or facial expression perhaps, may be transformed into a device for action. Even proper names may fall under this category. Such preludes as "Washington says . . . ," "Pushkin says . . . ," and "Tagore says . . ." are frequently cited not so much to bring to light what these individuals believe but to coax others to embrace the opinion stated through the weight of authority. In this respect we are frequently impressed with the apparent effectiveness of some of the current approaches on ideological disputations. A most appealing defense of one's own position, it seems, is to advance the endorsement of a person or an institution which is not assailable for other reasons. The eloquence of action language joins the head of the speaker with the heart of the listener. Action is incurred without the obstacle of thought.

Poetic language induces a mood. We observe its charm in a poem, a symphony, a painting, a ballet. It stresses the quality of emotions rather than the utility of experience. The difference between descriptive and poetic language can be illustrated by Eddington's example: If we are concerned with the formation of waves by winds in the physics laboratory, we had best look up the standard descriptive hydrodynamic equations beginning with

$$\frac{p'_{vv}}{g\rho\eta} = \frac{(\alpha^2 + 2\nu k\alpha + \sigma^2)A - i(\sigma^2 + 2\nu km\alpha)C}{gk(A-iC)}$$

The series of equations go on to show that winds of less than half a mile an hour leave the surface of the water unruffled. As the speed rises to a mile an hour, minute corrugations appear. Finally, gravity waves are produced at wind speeds of two miles an hour. Yet were we strolling along the shore, the same thought of the generation of waves by winds might evoke sentiments much more aptly described by Rupert Brooke:

> There are waters blown by changing winds to laughter
> And lit by the rich skies all day and after
>   Frost with a gesture stays the waves that dance,
> And wandering loneliness; he leaves a white
> Unbroken glory, a gathered radiance,
> A width, a shining peace, under the night.

The composition of poetic language varies greatly. In poetry the context cannot be divorced from the verse, the melody, and the rhythm. The pleasing euphony and the elliptical words blend with the sensuous beauty of the metered sounds. In painting, elements more direct than words are used to communicate a momentary sliver of eternity. The experience of the view is coordinated with the practical experience lying outside it. Words originated as a mimicry of sounds; painting began as an imitation of the outside world. Leonardo da Vinci speaks of the painter and the sculptor as the great teachers in the objective realms.

There are certain sensations—the woe of a wail, the serenity of a scene, the humor of a joke, the biting of a sarcasm, the devotion of a liturgy, the ecstasy of a song—that can only be suggested by poetic language. There is no direct statement. Yet what can be more explicit a portrayal of the profundity of human reasonableness than an essay of Montaigne, a sharing of deep sorrow than the Pietà of Michelangelo, a union with nature than a verse of Su Tung-po? Poetic language thus becomes descriptive language of another order.

Generally speaking poetic language is not pure in practice. Only music, or perhaps the more abstract paintings, like some works of Klee, Kandinsky, and Picasso can be considered strictly poetic. It is true that the lyrical aspects dominate in painting. Nevertheless, painting does retain a shade of the descriptive. El Greco could not have displayed his feelings concerning the city of Toledo without representing it on his magnificent canvas.

Conversely, descriptive words themselves are tinged with poetic harmonics. Except for mathematical symbols there are few completely descriptive terms. Meanings of words are muted by the conditions of learning and prior use. There are the personal sensibilities and dispositions toward the sounds and meanings, which color the descriptive sense. Such psychological connotations elicit subconscious reactions, and descriptive language is infected with action.

The ideal of unity in science has led many a positivist to search for a unified language. It did not appear proper that physics, chemistry, biology, sociology, and other disciplines should remain aloof from each other in a Babel of strange tongues. Surely if the methods, criteria of validity, and concepts are related, they should all mesh into a single pattern. A common code should be established. The individual schemes should become dialects which can be translated into the parent language with its universal system of signs and rules.

For a time philosophers like Carnap and Neurath believed that physics met the requirements. It was soon recognized that the language of physics has too narrow a base to include the qualitative predicates of the perceptual world. Carnap thereupon modified his original proposal into the "thesis of the reducibility of scientific language to the thing-language." Statements are to be converted into descriptions involving material objects. In the case of a tuning fork, for example, the auditory sense quality is to be translated into the physical description of vibration frequencies.

A big stumbling block to these attempts is the fate of psychological statements. Is the mental state an incommensurate world separate from the physical state? We are confronted with the same vigorous polemics which have baffled philosophers for thousands of years.

If a dualism is accepted, the thing-language falls down in universality. If a monism is accepted and psychology is considered a branch of physics, then meaningful psychological statements would appear to be reducible into the thing-language. However, this leads us nowhere but back into the vicious circle: The thing-language is considered valid as the language of unified science if mental statements that cannot be included into the system are eliminated as meaningless metaphysics.

As far as structure is concerned, our language is quite primitive. Words are taken simply as they are handed down by our ancestors. We do not seriously question whether or not the morphology of our inherited language corresponds to that of the real world of which is is symbolic.

Korzybski outlined the development of the anthropocentric concept of the world. Primitive mythology envisioned gods and demons in human shapes. These gods would go about constructing a world in a piecemeal fashion, much in the way a man would. A language was formulated to fit. It was given a subject-predicate form. Language and thought had a "plus" character. Beginning with something, one adds components to it. Even today's science feels at home more with an accretive and additive approach rather than a simultaneous aggregate apprehension.

One of the greatest barriers to drawing a consistent world picture lies in our acquired language, which is structurally incongruous with reality. During recent years the language problem has become widely recognized. For decades the Vienna Circle stressed the logical analysis of language as the main purpose of philosophy. The Circle tried to uncover the sources of recurrent absurdities and misconceptions. The question considered is not so much that a particular statement is false but that it is senseless. The analysis begins with intrinsic meanings. The actual experience that is expressed in a word, phrase, or theory must be uncovered in order to examine the nature of discourse.

Studies on the substance of language showed that Newtonian concepts no longer have the meanings once ascribed to them. What was said in Newton's days was not even an accurate description of the relevant operations. This led the logical empiricists to advance a criterion of factual meaningfulness. According to Bridgman's operational analysis, the key to the meaning of a concept is given by the corresponding set of operations. The meaningful term must be relatable to some concrete process, event, or object, so that verification can be forthcoming. Otherwise we are just dealing in phantom verbiage. The physicist must therefore concentrate on the application of terms to operationally defined propositions. He pays particular attention to insuring that the expressions are used in the way he thinks they are. This requires a clear conception of the designations with respect to performable operations. The conditions of the experiments as well as the methods of measurements are to be outlined.

There are some reservations to the rigid adoption of this approach in practice. The number of terms that would require operational clarity is staggering. Only relatively few are susceptible to even a crude dissection of this nature. In the meantime the only tools available are words and symbols, not yet related semantically to realizable operations.

Furthermore, operational analysis does not escape metaphysics, which it professes to do. A term or symbol is simply a sign representing some thing, some operation, or some event. To be meaningful this thing, operation, or event must exist. Thus, the term "food" presupposes the existence of living beings capable of eating. This slides us back into the metaphysical pit of existence in which operational analysis becomes a close neighbor of metaphysics.

Although a language can be revised somewhat from within, it cannot be drastically improved or modified except by means of some new leverage outside itself. A language cannot definitively describe itself; another with a different structure must be used. In order to improve the old Euclidian and Newtonian systems, for example, Einstein had to develop an entirely new vocabulary and thought structure. It is this structural advantage that provides the freshness of the viewpoint of the stranger, the consultant, and the confidant.

Because of the incongruity of the structure of language to reality, there are many bugaboos that bear watching. One results from the belief in the existence of qualities simply because words have been invented to represent them. This is exemplified by the question: Where is the hole after you have eaten the doughnut? It is easy to see how this came about. Since the world is complex and beyond the simultaneous grasp of our simple minds, we are forced to break it into neat little comprehensible packages. While examining one of these, we assume through wishful thinking that the others would remain fixed. For practical purposes within careful limits, this supposed constancy is frequently useful.

Take the simple example: Jackson the man. To a physicist, Jackson is a mass of whirling protons, electrons, and other nuclear particles undergoing continuous exchange with the surroundings. To a biologist he is a succession of biochemical transformations and physiological processes. In any case Jackson is not a static object. His ideals are continually being modified; his muscles are persistently being broken down and rebuilt; his beard is daily being shaved. Within a year the bulk of his body tissues are renewed through metabolic changes. The poet Auden described our Jacksons thus:

> . . . we die
> Each moment and that each great I
> Is but a process in a process
> Within a field that never closes;
> As proper people find it strange
> That we are changed by what we change
> That no event can happen twice
> And that no two existences
> Can be alike;

We never have an immutable conception of Jackson. We merely coin his stable name for an actually unstable object. We observe a general similarity between Jackson and other approximations, all of whom we classify as men. The assumption of a fixed reality may be useful in everyday life. However, we must be careful with cases such as the hole in the doughnut. Even with a distinct name the hole does not have a separate and constant being. It disappears with the first bite.

Attempting to hold things constant while shifting one or two variables at a time is common in experimental science. Boyle's law, for example, stipulates that at a constant temperature, the volume of a gas varies inversely as the pressure. If we merely follow the words, the three entities of temperature, pressure, and volume are given individual existences. In reality this is not so and more people are recognizing the fact. Physicists have led the way. Mass is fused with energy, space with time, cause with effect. In the biological sciences too we are witnessing a gradual cognizance of the unreality of atomic separations, such as the waning controversy in genetics concerning the effects of germ plasm versus environment.

We often permit the inferences from words to have an objective being in our subconscious. This practice is called absolutism. The English "to be" implies a distinct existence for the adjective. When we say "Saunders is tall and handsome," we imply that there are such things in the universe as tallness and handsomeness. The qualities are to have a cosmic substance. A logical misconception of the same nature was neatly expressed by Lewis Carroll in "Through the Looking Glass." Alice remarked, "I see nobody on the road." "I only wish *I* had such eyes," the king rejoined, "to be able to see *nobody* and at that distance too!"

The Indo-European language tends to corral thought in divisions of black and white rather than shades of gray. To minimize the resulting misunderstandings scientists have substituted measurements for absolute terms. Instead of saying that the weather is hot, which actually means hot relative to our own sensations, we say that the temperature is 110 ° Fahrenheit. The personalized aspects are thereby reduced in scientific descriptions. Absolutes are more common in nontechnical usage. Words such as rich and poor, fast and slow, sweet and sour continue to invite the dangers of absolutism. It may well be that the acceptable error surrounding their usage in everyday life is so wide that we do not require a finer precision of expression. In times of critical debate, however, we must recognize the vagueness of language and not press the issue beyond its limits. There are always variations about which we cannot verbalize decisively.

The misapplication of symbols needs some attention. Symbols may have meaning under one set of circumstances and not under another. For example, while the temperature of a mass of molecules comprising a pint of water can be known, that for a single molecule has no meaning. Temperature is a function of the vibrations of molecules against each other. The proper context for meaningfulness in this instance requires at least two molecules.

Another fallacy is confounding the orders of abstraction. In the effective use of language the same level must be maintained throughout the discourse. Words are abstractions of things and inferences are abstractions of words. Ambiguity occurs when inferences are taken for the spoken words and words are taken for the real things. Every word, sentence, or doctrine is based on certain postulates. Shifting the level of abstraction, while using the same words, actually involves an unwarranted change of premises.

Many questions are meaningless because of empty postulates. Let us take an example: Why should you obey the authority of any government? The question is tantamount to asking whether or not there can be a political unit without political obligations. This is stretching language beyond its presuppositional elasticity.

As listeners unwary executives are frequently charmed by the persuasiveness of the speaker. In an age of specialization, eloquence camouflaging for truth is a recurring source of misjudgments. It is relatively easy for a specialist gifted in the artifice of action language to mislead the average audience. For this reason the executive must develop a keen insight for penetrating the sonorous forensics into the inner shrine of the argument. Only when versed in such an intuitive skill will he be able to disregard the froth of the scientific peddler and observe the relations of unvarnished facts.

Yet the executive himself deals in action language to further his objectives. He must maintain the morale of the laboratory; he must raise financial support; he must publicize the group; he must assuage grievances; he must convince the opposition; he must recruit researchers. All of these responsibilities imply the stratagem of action language. This is especially applicable in a country where six and a half billion dollars or forty-two dollars per capita were spent in 1951 on advertisements. On the one hand, the executive seeks the facts and not the salesmanship. On the other hand, he himself is tempted to rely on the perfume of rhetoric.

If the executive demands unadorned and factual statements from his associates, should he not reciprocate likewise? In the face of losing his just share of the market, should he remain purely descriptive before customers and judges who are unable to distinguish integrity among competing presentations? Does his obligation to obtain proper financial support for his staff justify a colored exaggeration of their contributions to the patrons? Should the public be deceived for the public good? We will leave these questions to the reader's own taste and conscience.

A pleasant confession of resorting to action language was written by Lord Chesterfield to his son. In the eighteenth century, England together with Russia and Sweden continued to follow the Julian calendar, which was off eleven days a year. The Catholic powers in Europe had already adopted the more accurate Gregorian calendar. Lord Chesterfield therefore introduced the appropriate bill before parliament for the change in England. He wrote, ". . . I determined, therefore, to attempt the reformation; I consulted the best lawyers and the most skilful astronomers, and we cooked up a bill for that purpose. But then my difficulties began: I was to bring in this bill, which was necessarily composed of law jargon and astronomical calculations, to both of which I am an utter stranger. However, it was absolutely necessary to make the House of Lords think that I knew something of the matter; and also to make them believe that they knew something of it themselves, which they do not. For my own part, I could just as soon have talked Celtic or Slavonian to them, as astronomy, and they would have understood me full as well; so I resolved better than speak to the purpose, and to please instead of informing them. I gave them, therefore, only an historical account of calendars, from the Egyptian down to the Gregorian, amusing them now and then with little episodes; but I was particularly attentive to the choice of my words, to the harmony and roundness of my periods, to my elocution, to my action. This succeeded and ever will succeed; they thought I informed, because I pleased them; and many of them said, that I had made the whole very clear to them, when God knows, I had not even attempted it."

In the light of the many pitfalls of language and in our inclination toward verbosity we should take profitable heed from the old Chinese scholars. They were not impressed with the phrase "logical necessity." They distrusted logic because of a matured lack of faith in words and definitions. The more they tried to define their terms, the more terms they had to define in order to define their terms in a quest for the impossible logical perfection. Sooner or later their chase ended with undefined phrases and a leap had to be made then to experience.

Rather than spend our lives in the pursuit of words and definitions beyond their intrinsic limits, we should dwell in the suggestive fullness of workable terms. Let the range and beauty of life pass into our minds as an echo of man-made definitions. "Words need have only enough stability of meaning," says F. C. S. Schiller, "to yield a sufficient clue to the new senses to be conveyed, to render the latter intelligible, in their context, not in the abstract." Accordingly, scholars recognize the effective reaches of symbols and language. When they work in the domain of science, they use the fitting medium of words and logic. But when they play in the realm of pure conversation lying beyond shapes and features—to anticipate Chapter 9—they do not trivialize the content by, as Shelley puts it, "a shroud of talk to hide us from the sun of this familiar life." "The Sage does not talk; the Talented Ones talk; the Stupid Ones argue": this is an old Oriental adage. By not stretching words beyond their substantial worth, the sage avoids their deceptiveness.

The executive should always remember that it was Mephistopheles who gave the following advice:

> Above all else rely on words;
> Then you can pass through the safe gate
> Into the temple of all certainty,
> Where even ideas are wanting
> A timely word will serve as well.

Appropriate warning against this seduction had long ago been given by the Dai-O-Kohuski:

> Wishing to entice the blind
> The Buddha playfully let word escape from his golden mouth;
> Heaven and earth are filled, ever since, with entangling briars.

And if the good Christian prefers a mandate from a more familiar authority, he may turn his ear to the voice of the Lord, as it had come down from the clouds to Job in his scepticism, "Who is this that darkened counsel by words without knowledge?"

Chapter 8

Abstraction

MAN OBVIOUSLY CANNOT GRASP the universe in one fell swoop. In order to even begin to comprehend the world around us, we usually resort to breaking out little segments for observation one at a time. Scientific knowledge is gained through such an analytic procedure. Before we become too enthusiastic about treating human beings in a "scientific manner," managing companies on a "scientific basis," operating the government in a "scientific fashion," or organizing our lives through a "scientific approach," as many are now urging, we should explore this abstractive scaffolding of the scientific method.

⌈By treating things in the abstract, we mean that they are comprehensible without reference to some other item.⌉ Being abstract transcends concrete occasions, although this does not necessarily imply that the dissociated thing and the enveloping context are not connected. The degree of abstraction may vary. We may be more or less restrictive. For example, we progressively extend the abstractiveness as we proceed along the following series: baseball player, athlete, man, animal, and life.

Complex objects are regarded as those which can be analyzed into relationships involving eternal components. Simple ones cannot. Whitehead explains how the realm of eternal objects can be dissected into a series of grades of simple and complex eternal objects.

By continuing along the successive tiers of increasing intricateness in the area of possibilities, an abstractive hierarchy can be constructed. The components begin with a simple eternal object as the base. Each level is connected with the other by a common set of their members. These groupings may be finite or infinite depending upon when they stop in their progression.

In a finite abstractive hierarchy there is a point of maximum complexity. The constituent in that position is not found in any other rung of the ladder. Beginning with any complex eternal object as the vertex of a finite abstractive pyramid we can by an analytical breakdown of components find one component in a lower echelon. Through successive steps of this sort we finally reach the simple object which forms the base. Since we are dealing in this case with possibilities, these eternal objects retain their isolation. There is no overlapping among them.

In mathematical abstractions, as Korzybski points out, all particulars are included. The definition of a circle as the locus of all points in a plane equidistant from a point called the center is complete. Mathematics provides us with a fictitious, simplified, verbal world which is not encountered in its pure form in nature.

In nature, the eternal objects are interlaced in a most intimate fashion. This interrelatedness in actuality leads to an infinite abstractive hierarchy, in which all members are involved. It is impossible to describe an actual situation exhaustively. There is associated with it a limitless chain of concepts with all degrees of complexity. From this we can see that an abstraction from actuality is considerably different from that from possibility, described in the previous three paragraphs. In the abstraction from actuality we are closer to the concrete situation when we turn to an event with a higher grade of complexity in the associated hierarchy. There is an infinite intermingling. We are continually reminded of this assertion in our daily activities.

Let us take a stroll through a gallery. There the works of art, which have been withdrawn from their original settings—a king's palace, a prince's tomb, a Buddhist temple, a Greek garden, a conquered home— are now bolted to strange pedestals or hung in gilded frames amidst alien surroundings. To be sure, even in these orphanages they radiate charm and beauty. The Winged Victory mounted on a landing above flights of marble stairs under high vaulted ceilings, commanding one of the principal approaches in the Louvre and directing all attention to herself, as it were, is a beautiful sight indeed. But it is a shrunken appreciation of her intrinsic art, if our imagination stops at the abstractive limits of museum settings. The living art of the Winged Victory can only be grasped if our minds flow back to the Samothracian days when she proudly commemorated the gallant naval victory in her post on a cliff overlooking the sea. The handling of a Louix XV tabatière should recall the graceful minuets and elegant gestures of his unbathed and pock-marked friends in fine trappings. In the succinct words of Malraux, art museums are pageants "not of color but of pictures, not of sculpture but of statues."

Let us look at industry. Companies cannot survive out of their social surroundings. To talk about a concern detached from customers is like speaking of a fish out of water. Barnard clearly demonstrated that the totality of an industrial organization must not only include investors, employees, and suppliers but also the clientèle. Through the act of purchasing, customers share in the seller's organization in a seller-buyer relationship. They are brought into collaboration through the same selling methods as are employees. Inducing the customer to trade his money for services is not fundamentally different from convincing the worker to exchange his services for money. Maintaining the shopper's good will is not different from keeping up the employee's morale. The education of customers is as strenuously pursued as that of workers. Deterrents and inducements to buyers are exerted by price adjustments, courtesy of treatment, and convenience of services. The same general techniques are used in the supervision and inspection of customers and employees. Bank and market analysts specialize in the evaluation of clients.

Let us turn to the legal picture. In law we are forced to admit the necessity of social acquiescence, apart from which justice becomes unenforceable. As Justice Wiley Rutledge points out, "Justice cannot be embalmed in the mores of any day or age. Nor can law." As a result of its history, tradition, and environment a society evolves certain behavior patterns. Out of these, standards of propriety are adopted by the community. From the approved norms, the law is derived with its sequence of apparatus and procedures. In theory, justice is strict and immutable. But in life, it is contingent and approximate.

Let us select still other cases from our ordinary experience. We find a continuing practice of extracting a "representative" sample or "type" species in our day-to-day conversations. When we talk about the "Greeks" of the fourth century B. C., for example, we usually mean the Athenians. We do not include the Spartans, Thebans, or even the poor Athenians and slaves.

Even the meaning of such elementary entities as words cannot be grasped fully except in the context in which they appear. As a separate entry in the dictionary, each word has several meanings. To determine which of the alternatives prevails, the sentence in which it stands must be taken into account. If we wish to delve into still finer shades and nuances, we must study the mannerisms of the author. The matter of intent and malice aforethought as inferred from words has been the bone of endless contention between crafty attorneys before learned judges for centuries.

Sometimes even "facts" are regarded as abstractions and are accordingly employed. F. E. Johnson tells the story about a Welshman's answer to a query about the character of Lloyd George. "Well," he answered, "I'll tell you. He's the sort of man that won't stand any nonsense from some d— fact." Johnson goes on to suggest that "imaginative devices in communications are justified when, though they take liberties with the cold facts, they are effectual means of conveying vital truth."

We are led by this short discussion of abstraction to the conclusion that there is exactness only in theory. Living experiences are always approximations of becoming.

Casual observers may object to the ostracism of exactitude from life. They may insist on the apparent correspondence between exact arithmetic computations and exact arithmetic observations. They say we observe just one tree—no more, no less. Yet have we observed precisely? Suppose we are pinned down to trillionth of a millimeter; then where does the tree leave off and the inanimate world begin? When does the molecule of carbon dioxide, the diameter of which is in the order of one ten millionth of a millimeter, become part of the living chloroplast in the process of being absorbed? When are the water molecules leaving the stomata of the leaves no longer a component of the cells? How about the falling twigs, the salts being drawn from the soil by the fine root hairs, the rosin oozing from the delicate cells in the bark? In actuality, therefore, we observe only an abstraction as a general appearance and structure of a tree. There is no preciseness. It is always a question of how much error one can afford under the circumstances.

Despite Whitehead's keen hierarchical analysis, most scientists follow Aristotle's classification approach. Objects are searched for common properties. Those exhibiting like characteristics are gathered together. The universe is considered the summation of assemblages of similar items. Mathematicians have grouped the twoness of mangos with the twoness of bananas into the mathematical class of twoness. Physicists have designated some score of nuclear particles depending on their mass, charge, and origin. Chemists have collected material into some hundred elements, according to their weight, reactivity, structure, and other properties. Biologists have divided living things into plant and animal kingdoms according to morphological and physiological features. Kingdoms are successively split into phyla, orders, families, genera, and finally species. The multimillion species are further subdivided into races, varieties, and strains.

The classification technique has considerable experimental value. Had this device not been developed, scientific progress would have been drastically retarded. As Poincaré surmised, "Suppose that instead of eighty elements we had eighty million and that they were not some common and others rare but uniformly distributed. Then each time we picked up a new pebble there would be a strong probability that it was composed of some unknown substance. Nothing that we knew about other pebbles would tell us anything about it." Order is the threshold of clarity. Classification is the tool for ordering.

But we should not expect too much from classification as a means of clarifying the ultimate character of things. When we press it too far, we run the risk of forgetting that our bunches and species are not bunches and species in the real world. They are merely snatches of mental aids. To foist them upon nature would render us insensitive to her continuum of delicateness and gradualness. This is the danger in scientific specialism, which frequently lapses into false abstractionism. How frequently do we hear: "If we can break man down into his basic components and study these individually, we will know what makes him tick?" Complicated processes are chopped like stew and scattered among specialists to boil away for decades. Man has been typed into upper, middle, and lower classes; or pyknic (round), asthenic (thin), and athletic (muscular); or tough-minded and tender-minded; or Dionysian and Apollonian. Human drives have been segregated into id, ego, superego; love into sexual, dermal, cardiac-respiratory, and unclassifiable. Economics has been divided into capital and labor. In literature too, we have been attracted to the neat and pithy phrases of Pascal, La Rochefoucauld, Samuel Johnson, and Lichtenberg. They have the appealing façade of simple packaged truths.

The skilful employment of abstractions is no mean task even in the physical sciences. But when we step into the world of living organisms we encounter almost insurmountable obstacles. There are more variables to be considered. There are strange factors coming into play. The organism adapts itself to new influences so that the time-halted abstractions cannot be refitted into its former setting. When we observe social behavior the task is almost too formidable for our squinting minds. The abstracted creatures think and outsmart our own abstractions.

Let us consider the position of man. He has a wide range of activities. He may simultaneously be a member of several societies. He may be a communicant of a certain church. At the same time he may share membership in the same labor union with adherents of different religions. Then there are the fraternities, the alumni associations, the community affairs, the political affiliations. As a participant in these various parties, man's allegiance is splintered hither and yon, depending upon the particular purpose and activity of the various groups at the given time. Occasionally, the demands of these fragmentary loyalties are mutually exclusive. As Max Otto has said, "It is not only because of their endless variety that men are baffling. Each individual is baffling."

In contrast to mere organisms, society anticipates a future and guides its own evolution out of past customs. In this development society is not dominated by a single will but by the many wills of constituents who are at the same time somewhat independent of it. It is through this modicum of independence that man, although a product of the community, is also a shaper of social character.

Despite the deceptive dangers attending the use of abstractions, many thinkers continue to single out one factor as the controlling agent in the life of individuals and communities. Freud emphasizes the sexual instinct; Nietzsche, the will to power; Marx, the economic desire. Powerful trends have been generated by these cogitations, and the world is still in the throes of responding to their undercurrents.

The wide latitude of discernment among human beings is a consequence of the varying manner in which they abstract from identical situations. As discussed in the previous chapter, the same word does not elicit exactly the same meaning in two persons. The final outcome lies in the light of the individual's own experience and not in the word itself. Because of this discrepancy, hair-splitting arguments over definitions are foredoomed to sterility. Yet this very subjectivity is a rich source of inspiration for the artist. Each painter of the same landscape provides a personal vivification of the fleeting physiognomy. His impressions of the forebodings of the misty shadows, of the liveliness of the cascading brook, of the restfulness of the rolling hills are his own. He intuitively knows that the pretended definitiveness of abstracted views is illusory. He accepts the impossibility of precision and remains exhilarated by the inexhaustibility of honest art in real life.

Unlike the artist the scientist continues to press the agreement of abstractions. One of the most interesting examples concerns the reconciliation of mental and physical processes. Descartes had separated the two, thereby influencing the path of science for ten generations. This basis for speculation had contributed greatly to the success of science. The dualism enabled science to tackle the simpler abstracted entities one by one and accordingly to make considerable material progress. Sooner or later, however, the reality of the dualism must be faced head on.

What is the relationship between a blow to the solar plexus and the sensation of a knockout? Between anxiety and stomach ulcers? Can physical agents generate mental processes operating in a separate domain? If they are one and the same event but viewed from different vantage points, there should be a common transformation factor, such as energy, related to a generally accepted scientific law, such as the conservation of energy. But were such the case, how would we go about measuring the energy involved in mental processes? We would soon be pushed into the circuitous assumption that mental operations involve nonmeasurable amounts of energy.

If we proceed along the dualistic attack, we would attempt to find the edge of discontinuity between mental and physical properties. But as we descend the ladder of the animal and the plant kingdoms, at what point does a given mental character disappear? Does an ass exercise free will when it refuses to budge? Does the plant show mental activity as it winds its tendrils around the supporting trellis and twists its shoots toward the light? Does the virus emulate the stoicism of the mystic? Here again, we find no means of conclusive differentiation.

Planck grappled with this dilemma. What is the relation between the physical wound of pricking with a needle and the mental sensation of pain? Both phenomena can be examined most exhaustively. Planck insists that the methods of analysis are mutually exclusive. The one on pain is directed toward one's mental reactions; the other on the wound toward the external world. Attempts to substitute one for the other lead only to confusion. Either physical or mental events exist but never physical and mental. Planck concluded that the body-mind question is a phantom problem. He contented himself with the expedient that it does no harm to say that the physical and the mental are just two views of the same phenomenon.

In contrast to Planck's compromise, philosophers like Whitehead feel that this estrangement of the body from the mind is the very blindness of science. By refusing to fuse mentality as an ingredient of nature, physical science does not add content to the notion of bare activity. Were it not for the mental aspects, the understanding of the activities of sociological entities in the world would be impossible. Aim is typically one such determinant, as is the case of motives in a first degree murder. Estimation of the defense potential of a nation is not merely an evaluation of her physical assets; it includes a determination of the will of her citizenry to fight. In all of these cases there is a mental directive conjoined to the physical. This motivation does not pause to entertain the dispute of mental versus physical realms. What happens happens as one act.

Ryle also stresses the unreality of the dualistic mental-physical world of Descartes. Ryle claims it to be a category mistake, which is illustrated by the following story: A visitor to a university was shown the laboratories, the dormitories, the library, the classrooms, and the rest of the campus. Upon the completion of the tour, he appeared perplexed and inquired of his guide: "I've seen where the experiments are carried out, where the students live and study, where the bills are paid and all that. But where is the university?" The guide had to explain that the university is not another collateral institution. It is simply the coordinated working of all he saw. It does not belong in the same category as the constituent departments. Ryle goes on to show that it is a family of radical mistakes of this type that is responsible for the dualism of Descartes which envisions a mental ghost ensconced within a physical machine.

Distortion is an ever present danger in viewing phenomena in abstraction. A journalistic example is the pet editorializing on modern science as the prime cause of current destructiveness in world conflicts. Science and destruction are lifted out of context in the human scene and the direct abstracted relationship is assumed as real. The fact that hostilities have existed throughout the history of man and that all talents have been marshaled in support of these affairs has been too lightly considered. We may recall Archimedes, who lent his scientific mind to assist the tyrant of Syracuse in defending the city against the Romans in the year 212 B. C. There were Leonardo da Vinci's contributions to the art of fortification for the Duke of Milan, Galileo's calculations of the trajectory of cannon balls for the Duke of Tuscany, and Faraday's consultations on the use of poison gases in the Crimean War. In Napoleon's invasion of Egypt hundreds of chemists, archaeologists, astronomers, and other technical personnel were brought along.

Neither has modern science been the instigator behind the sadism, cruelty, and viciousness that often reveal themselves in wars. What modern conflict can match the disaster of the Thirty Years War in the early 1600s that reduced the population of Central Europe from eighteen million to four? What modern battles can compare with the merciless butchering of the populations of conquered cities and towns during the rampage of Genghis Khan in the early 1200s? What modern records can rival the bloodiness of the Persian royalties following the days of Xerxes? Xerxes was murdered by the courtier, Artabanus, in 464 B. C. Artabanus in turn was killed by Artaxerxes I who was succeeded by Xerxes II. After a reign of a few weeks Xerxes II was assassinated by his half brother, Sogdianus, who, in turn, was slaughtered six months later by Darius II. When Terituchmes revolted, Darius II had him killed, his wife chopped into pieces, and his mother, brothers, and sisters buried alive. Darius II was followed by his son, Artaxerxes II, who had to kill his brother, Cyrus, in a battle for the throne. During his reign, Artaxerxes II executed his son Darius for conspiracy, only to die brokenhearted upon learning that another son, Ochus, was scheming to kill him. Ochus, in turn, was murdered during his reign by his own general. And so the terrible annals continued for a couple of hundred years.

Thus plunder and cruelty long antedated modern science. In relation to the capacity of populations to recover, earlier warfare has exhibited far greater ruthlessness. [Cessation of wars is a function of the exhaustibility of the human desire to continue fighting or living. Since modern life is organically integrated with technicism and since the materalistic philosophies have placed exaggerated values on goods, the destruction of property and matériel alone may be sufficient to break the will of present-day peoples to carry on the struggle. | In this way, much less suffering may need to be inflicted on human life itself before the cry for an armistice sets in. This is contrasted to the older days of simpler cultures when life was not enmeshed with the complicated machinery of specialized services and materials. Under those circumstances the loss of good alone might not be sufficient to bring about a collapse of resistance. In any case the loose charge that the wanton butchery of human beings is a direct result of modern scientific advancement is unfounded. Something else is Satan's emissary.

To recapitulate, there are no exact measurements in real life. Attempts to dissect and measure by means of abstractions fail in precision. Yet our own consciousness operates in practice by dwelling on finite chips from the infinite actuality. This procedure is necessary for discursive thought. It is the tool of the scientist.

To reverse the process of estimating life from dead abstractions and of transforming analysis into actuality is the art of the philosopher. A masterly extrapolation can provide a suggestiveness of the rounded wholeness unmatched by the most voluminous and detailed treatise on the subject. It recalls the advice of Anton Chekhov to his brother:

> In descriptions of nature one must seize on small details, grouping them so that when the reader closes his eyes, he gets a picture. For instance, you'll have a moonlit night if you write that on the mill dam a piece of glass from a broken bottle glittered like a bright little star.

Part III

Injection

of

an

Oriental

Outlook

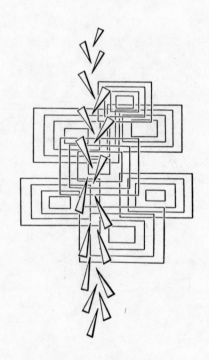

Chapter 9

No-Knowledge

THE LAST FIVE CHAPTERS discussed the presupposition underlying science that reason is the only medium for understanding. There may be other wellsprings of enlightenment. But priding himself on his rational mind, many a scientist is reluctant to rely on these less obvious avenues. At best, he may attempt to rationalize whether or not these alternate approaches to knowledge and truth are possible. But to judge something that lies beyond reason by means of reason itself does not appear reasonable. Would it not be wiser to refrain from prejudging the existence of phenomena beyond our rational comprehension? Should we not accept the other sources of knowledge for what they can provide until we do understand? After all, scientists are a mite superstitious themselves, if we care to put the proposition thus. They *do* believe in baffling unknowns; they *do* have faith in the existence of things beyond the compass of their current knowledge. Otherwise where do their research problems originate and why is the unknown pursued so vigorously? It is not without subconscious reason that we call many an unwarranted justification of an act "rationalizing."

In the consideration of extra-rational ramifications one of the first questions that comes to mind is: Is science a public or a private affair? Most scientists say public. These individuals dissociate themselves from artists on the basis of the claim that scientific knowledge can be communicated between people. In contrast, art is not supposed to appeal to universal assent. A deaf man, for example, cannot appreciate the harmony of a quartet, yet he can readily master the scientific theory of sound.

Bridgman represents a departure from the fold. He contends that science is a personal estate. One's sensation is felt by oneself and not by society at large. Applying his operational analysis, he argues that the steps justifying the expression "my tooth aches" are different from those involved in the saying "your tooth aches." However, the linguistic habits into which we have settled suppress the operational differences between the two. Compounding them into "Does your toothache feel like my toothache?" is considered a pseudo-question. There are many instances in which one feels experience of his own and not that of others. Yet the reverse can also occur. Thus one would be hard put to determine his own death operationally. But he can sense the death of another.

Everyone may concur on the number of kumquats in a jar and on the specific location on a numbered scale at which a particular line of light comes to rest. But activities of this kind do not comprise the substance of science. The quiddity lies in the theories which explain the observations. There may be consensus on the wave length with which a certain light is correlated. But there is far less agreement on the hypotheses regarding the nature of that light or its appearance at that specific position in the spectrum.

Science excludes the majority of the people from voting because of their unfamiliarity with the subject at hand. How does this practice differ from that of the poet who chooses to ignore readers insensible to the metric beauty of his lines? Even if voices are limited to the informed, the conclusions are still far from unanimous. Despite the popular judgment of his contemporaries the great chemist Faraday opposed the atomic theory. Einstein was in the minority among modern physicists with regard to certain extensions of his relativity principle. Then too, the "public" of which science speaks is limited to egoistic man. The fact that animals and plants have been disfranchised is overlooked in the grand pretensions of the universality of science.

There are many questions which cannot be proven by referendum.

It is meaningless for a group of people to argue against one of its members who claims to have seen God among them. How can the group decide whether God was present or that the person was deluded into believing so?

A more earthly example involves the taste of ancient eggs. It is idle to discuss whether the difference in acceptance by two individuals is due to their divergent preferences concerning the same physical taste sensation or to the inducement of different physical taste sensations by the same eggs. Such arguments degenerate quickly into mere rhetoric.

It appears that science is claiming an oversimplified distinction from the arts. Actually the supposed freedom from subjectivity is only a matter of degree. Art may strive more conscientiously than science for such subjective qualities as harmony and beauty. Yet the quest for truth is not a stranger to the arts. It has a deep bearing in literature. Concepts are embodied in poetry in several ways. They may not appear as explicit statements but nevertheless may exist as an over-all connotation. Norris Weitz interpreted the thesis of Eliot's *Prufrock* to be that there are two kinds of life and two kinds of death. Yeats' *A Deep-sworn Vow* argues that the memory of true love cannot be erased. In the analysis of paintings, Erwin Panofsky stresses his belief that not only are single truth claims pursued in the works of such painters as Watteau and Poussin, but entire truth systems. With these two artists the complete theme of transience is analyzed with reference to the death theme intermeshed with the cyclical succession, subordinating the individual to the inexorable cosmic laws.

Furthermore, science herself is not beyond the caresses of subjective pleasures. It is the aesthetic embellishments of the harmonious patterns of scientific theories that provide much of their appeal. One mathematical solution is frequently preferred over another on the grounds of its "elegance." In *A Mathematician's Apology* G. H. Hardy considered seriousness and beauty as criteria of mathematical excellence. Dorothy Walsh applied the two criteria equally to art. By seriousness is meant "depth and universality"; by beauty is meant "unexpectedness combined with inevitability and economy."

The Indian Samkara maintains that in observing things we not only perceive our perceptions but something which is neither ourselves nor our perceptions. Taoists are imbued with a feeling of man's pervasive union with nature. Proponents of Thomistic philosophy say that knowledge is becoming immaterially the thing known. This knowledge is not acquired through concepts or reason but is inborn or inherently given. It includes the moral knowledge of the virtuous man, the mystical knowledge of the saint, and the poetic knowledge of the artist. We observe distant reflections of the same type of awareness in the batting of a Di Maggio at the baseball plate, the cueing of a Hoppe at the billiard table, and the military estimate of a Lee on the field of battle.

It is understandable why such beliefs implying an amorphous source of enlightenment may be repugnant to a thoroughgoing rationalist. Their origins appear biased and subjective. Actually reason itself is not impartial. Each system of thought, whether Protestant or Catholic, Republican or Democratic, scientific or poetic, has its own rationale. It is as impossible to appeal to a neutral principle to determine the rationality of competing systems, as it is to invoke a neutral vocabulary to characterize a language. It is in the name of one kind of logic that one rejects the logic of another. Arnold Nash illustrated this "irrational prejudice" of reason very well in the story of a doctoral examination. The candidate, who submitted a study on Mormon history, was asked whether he, being a Mormon, regarded himself sufficiently unprejudiced to write a thesis on Mormon history. The student replied, "Yes, if you, not a Mormon, consider yourself unprejudiced enough to examine it."

Even among hardened skeptics we find a lapsing usage of the terms: predisposition, insight, vision, hunch, instinct, penetrating mind, imagination, feel, and intuition. The Upanishads long ago admonished against the inadequacy of the intellect. St. Augustine states: "I believe in order that I may understand." Coleridge calls it a "willing suspension of disbelief." These are indications of the subconscious obeisance that everyone pays to a hazy extrarational source of inspiration. They are the springboards of the anti-intellectual schools.

Anti-intellectualism suggests that rationality is weak as an instrument for human affairs. It points to a host of other influences on human thought: habits, reflexes, prejudices, appetites, passions, emotions. In the more extreme form involving romanticism, nonrationality is even exalted and feeling is preferred to thinking. In its more reasonable form, anti-intellectualism attempts to ascertain the proper application of rationality in human behavior. There are reasons and there are reasons. Henry

Aldrich, the dean of Christ Church in Oxford in the seventeenth century, rhymed it humorously for drinking:

> If on my theme I rightly think,
> There are five reasons why men drink:
> Good wine, a friend, because I'm dry;
> Or lest I should be by and by
> Or—any other reason why.

Pavlov's dogs are interesting in this respect. Conditioned reflexes were developed by training. The resulting automatic response of watering at the mouth at the associated sound of a bell in anticipation of food was essentially similar to inborn responses. The demonstrations were considered by anti-intellectuals as supporting the importance of factors other than rationality in human decisions.

Freud held that man's thoughts and desires are a compounded agglomerate. Only with the greatest of skill and difficulty can they be partially disentangled to determine why an individual did what he did. There are many things that a man does without undergoing a conscious and rational process. These may be actuated by conditioned reflexes, automatic drives, traditions, and all sorts of subconscious urges. The part played by ratiocinative thinking in the life of an individual is actually limited.

In their efforts to pass beyond the intellect, the Zen Buddhists have emphasized the experience of the moment. Deliberation should not be permitted to interfere with the immediacy of the response. Just as the sound does not wait to issue forth when the bell is struck, man should develop that consciousness of mind that focuses infinite experience into instant intuition. The spontaneity of reaction is stressed continuously by the Zen Master to his disciples. In the art of fencing the counter movements must be made without slow logic or hesitant reasoning. The intuition springs forth as a wordless and thoughtless message translated into integrated and immediate action. A striking impression can be gathered from the Sumiye school of painting. The spirit of Zen is marvelously expressed. The painting is executed on paper so thin that the slightest hesitancy will cause it to tear. The strokes are swift and decisive. They are final and irrevocable, like a castrated steer. There can be no retouching. The objects are always embodiment of movement depicting the becomingness of nature and the free expression of the intuitive spirit.

We may observe an inkling of a similar rapidity of response among our kith and kin of the animal world. The frog's tonguing a bee does not wait for the syllogisms. The spider spins a workable web the first time it tries. The weaver birds plait artistic nests even when kept for generations away from nesting material. These illustrations are not presented to press a Bergsonian similarity of human intuition to animal instinct. They are merely listed as further weights to the thesis that rational knowledge is not the only generative force behind reasonable actions.

Rational knowledge is rational only because it is obtainable through reason. The others obtainable through means other than reason are not irrational; they are extrarational. The gift of the gods is to recognize which is which—ideas that are susceptible to rational analysis and ideas that are not. For the executive, sensing the propriety of a particular intuitional judgment is as important as recognizing the soundness of a particular scientific proof.

Broadly speaking, intellectual progress is an advancement in concepts which man has formulated and handed down. But let us dissect the statement further. We should contrast rational knowledge and intuitive knowledge. The role of discovery is quite different in these two forms. In rational knowledge it plays a prominent part; this is where science has contributed greatly. In intuitive knowledge, discovery, of the patent office variety, plays a minor role. Science has not accelerated human development in this area. If anything, she may have dulled man's sensibilities to intuitive riches by her passive and in some instances antagonistic attitudes. All that is intuitively known has been recognized by persons living before, in other settings perhaps, but practiced to equal perfection. Political decisions in international statesmanship, maneuvers and countermaneuvers in military campaigns, estimates of the surges of people in elections, inspiration of poets, painters, and sculptors, conscience of holy men—all have been repetitiously exhibited through the ages. The great works of art of antiquity have never been surpassed or antiquated. The Ecclesiastes and Horace give as much enjoyment to us today as they did to the Hebrews and the Romans before Christ. The silent and formless depth of life had passed many times before the mind of man in its full sweep. This type of knowledge is not enkindled by mathematical formulae and scientific treatises. To pursue this latter means of communication is to remain in the realm of the rational. The inspiration can be shared only by those willing to accept the extrarational sources of enlightenment and keep the flow free from the dam of rational analysis.

Although much advance has been made in the analysis of rational knowledge, intuitive knowledge has not gained the same clarity of assertion and definition. While logic is susceptible to patterned discourse, intuition cannot be systematized in a comparable fashion. This realization tempted many people to regard rational knowledge and intuitive knowledge as opposing schools competing for disciples. Logicians deprecate the fuzziness of intuition; the intuitionists decry the strictures of logic. Actually, there is no exclusiveness of one over the other. Discursive reasoning is not possible without intuition. Consider Langer's example of the syllogism. To her syllogisms are merely devices to lead a person from one intuition to the next. The ability to react with intuitive understanding at each step is a prerequisite to rational analysis. The emergence of meaning is considered always a matter of logical intuition or insight. In real life this intuitive understanding is not built up step-by-step, as is the case with logical discourse. Instead it is grasped as an immediate total apprehension.

Yet even intuitive knowledge itself is not the ultimate stretch. Sooner or later we hesitate at the limits of rational and intuitive knowledge. Our faltering mind must then seek repose and cure in what it cannot know. At this point the concept of sage-knowledge or no-knowledge is introduced by the Taoists. This is really not knowledge in the ordinary sense. Knowledge, as we understand it in the West, involves the selection of a certain event or quality as the object of knowledge. Sage-knowledge does not do so. It concerns an understanding of what the East calls *Wu* or nonbeing. The *Wu* transcends events and qualities; it has no shape, no time. As a result it cannot be the object of ordinary knowledge. At the higher level of cognizance, the sage forgets distinctions between things. He lives in the silence of what remains in the undifferentiable whole.

[An important difference exists between "having-no" knowledge and having "no-knowledge." The former is merely a state of ignorance; the latter is one of ultimate enlightenment and universal sensibilities.] To the confirmed rationalist, no-knowledge may appear to be the hugger-muggery of the mystagogue. Nevertheless, it is precisely its ineffability that lends force to its reality. The mysteries of nature appear to be mysteries only to those who refuse to participate in them.

It is in this area of no-knowledge that all nature shares a kindred voice. Its utterance is not restricted to the rationality of one species nor to the grammar of one language. It is the reservoir of the evolutionary vestiges shared by all, as they differentiated into their respective genera and forms. There is something of primordial man in the fish; there is something of primordial fish in the man.

Man does not gain simplicity by leading the life of unlettered shepherds or by relinquishing his command of rational knowledge. He gains humility by widening his awareness of the vastness of nature through ungrudging communion with her. Man need not creep on all fours to share the naturalness of the animals, as rabid followers of Rousseau may suggest; he need only converse in the common domain of no-knowledge. It is the art of participation in these pastures that infuses the true zoologist with the deep feeling for the sentiments of animals, so that the observed creatures themselves speak through his data. It is no-knowledge that enables the true botanist to transfuse his own understanding empathetically into the plant kingdom, so that his works breathe through its stomata. It is this kindred spirit that enabled the illustrious Sung poet Lu Yu, to find sympathy for his own unsuccessful (to him) career in the plight of the neglected plum tree. With acknowledgment to Kuangchi Chang's translation, we read:

> By the broken bridge outside the courier station
> The plum tree blooms desolately, ownerless;
> When the dusk comes it is grieving yet,
> Irritated by the wind and the rain.

> It wishes not to compete for the spring's favor
> And gives way to other flowers' jealousy,
> Falling in the mud, ground to dust—
> Only its fragrance remains as ever.

It is no-knowledge that stimulates the Taoist artist to paint a forest "as it would appear to the trees themselves" and capture the "tigerishness of the tiger," thereby imparting a feeling of nature that is rarely equaled in Occidental paintings with their anthropocentric overcast.

With rational knowledge, the scientist is a spectator of nature. With no-knowledge, he becomes a participant in nature. There is a communion of understandings. He no longer shares that tragic suffering of many individuals, who "fear of finding oneself alone," as André Gide describes it, "and so they don't find themselves at all."

To quote the Zen Buddhists:

> An old pine tree preaches wisdom,
> And a wild bird is crying out truth.

Or from the concentrated fragments of the famous seventeenth century *samurai* Matsura Basho:

> The old pond,
> Aye, and the sound of a frog leaping into the water.

This aspiring oneness of man with nature, the universal theme of Taoist art, is vividly expressed by Su Tung-po of the eleventh century as he wrote about his painting of bamboos and rocks on his friend's wall:

> Receiving the moisture of wine,
> My intestines sprout and fork out,
> And from out my liver and lungs
> Shoot rocks and bamboos,
> Surging through my breast, irresistible,
> They find expression on your snow-white wall.

It is the lack of no-knowledge that prompts remarks such as those on the happiness of the goldfish in the bowl. As if the poor fish were ever asked! Or even worse, the cruel thoughtlessness of some biologists who would increase the number of animals to be sacrificed during an experiment to round figures of, say, 100, when perhaps 87 would have been statistically adequate, just for the sake of facility in averaging test results. As if the slight increase in the ease of calculations on the investigator's part were of greater moment to nature than thirteen lives!

This all-embracing applicability of no-knowledge makes it a valuable tool for the executive. It provides him with a common ground of all situations. It is his means of transcendence over specific experience of which he has not yet tasted. Versed in no-knowledge, he is at home under otherwise strange conditions; he always finds familiar strains in his management of assorted enterprises.

Integrity and humility pervade the realm of no-knowledge. There is no question of fame, by-lines, awards, titles, honors. There is only participation. Man does not know selflessness until he has shared no-knowledge with nature.

Creation in research is the fluorescence of no-knowledge. It is the reaching into this area of ineffability and pulling out its rational synonym in a form expressible in our human language. Transformation of one rational cog into another, adaptation of a theory to new systems, conversion of a hypothesis into practical hardware are not creative research. These are merely varieties of tautological research. Such accomplishments, we must hasten to add, are worthy pursuits. They forge the link between theory and utility, between laboratory dreams and human welfare. But they are not creative.

The average scientist regards creativity as an extension of rationality. Prevailing ideas of thermodynamics, quantum mechanics, enzyme-substrate complexes, and so on, are to be thrown like baited hooks into the ocean of knowledge. If this is repeated with sufficient persistence, some hitherto unknown may be hauled in by the lucky fisherman. But such is not the way of creativity. Rational hooks do not sink in the waters of no-knowledge. [To plumb the depths of no-knowledge, one must rely on his own ineffable awareness of the ineffable.] During this stage rational and factual knowledge is a hindrance and the investigator should keep his mind clear of it. He should try for the complete fusion of his own no-knowledge with the no-knowledge of the comprehended. Only after that ineffable union is affected is an attempt made to transfigure it into a conscious and rational analogue. Current rational knowledge is then tested for adaptability; new, conscious forms of expressions are developed; or the indescribable is left unmentioned. The capacity to realize these difficult syntheses is a rare endowment, and this is why creative genius comes seldom.

There has also been much groping in the West for this concept of no-knowledge. It is unfortunate, however, that considerable effort has been wasted in rationalizing no-knowledge or opposing it competitively with rational knowledge. This belief in the mutual exclusiveness of rational knowledge and no-knowledge traps us into thinking that the absence of one generates the presence of the other. This is not so. As described in Chapter 4, if we deal in such "truths of the common sense," we would lose all touch with "truths in the higher sense."

Surrealism as an art form has sought a new knowledge from the subconscious and irrational. Dreams with their mixed reality became a guidepost. In the paintings of Salvador Dali, we see peculiar mixtures of photographically accurate details and incongruous juxtapositions of corpses on the piano, sea shells as eyes, and sewing machines on dissecting tables. These paradoxes were meant to suggest a "second reality" and an inclusion of everything within the whole. The kinship between the subconscious of the surrealist and that of no-knowledge, however, is remote. The dogmatic, aggressive pursuit of the irrational in the former case stands in sharp contrast to the serene reflective passivity in the latter.

Sorokin's analysis of cognition may be taken as an introduction to the Taoist concept of no-knowledge. He recognizes three systems of truth. The first group of propositions deals with sensory aspects of the world. These are confined to the responses of sense organs and are known as Sensate Truth. The second group, or Rational Truth, is obtained through logic, reason, and the scientific method. The third group, or Ideational Truth, is superrational and supersensory. In this last group we may include the direct intuition, revelations, and sudden enlightenment of the Buddhists.

There is only a small departure from Sorokin's triad to the rational, intuitive, and no-knowledge triad presented in this chapter. The Sensate Truth of Sorokin is combined with his Rational Truth in our rational knowledge. Our intuitive knowledge and no-knowledge are possibly both implied by Sorokin in his Ideational Truth but are separated in our own treatment. In the present discourse intuitive knowledge is considered to be knowledge from a superrational source but generally limited to the human mind. It is an instantaneous integration of unexpressed human thought. No-knowledge is also superrational in origin but is not restricted to the human mind in conception. It is indigenous to all nature. Hence, no-knowledge is not a projection of one's ego into nature; it is nature's ego shared by all. It alone makes man actively intimate with nature. With rational knowledge, one is in tune with the scientific man; with intuitive knowledge added, one is in tune with the total man; with no-knowledge added, one is in tune with nature.

One of the best Taoist poems inspired by no-knowledge is that by T'ao Ch'ien of the fourth century. To borrow from Arthur Waley's translation:

79

> I built my hut in a zone of human habitation,
> Yet near me there sounds no noise of horse or coach,
>> Would you know how that is possible?
> A heart that is distant creates a wilderness around it.
> I pluck chrysanthemums under the eastern hedge,
> Then gaze long at the distant summer hills.
> The mountain air is fresh at the dusk of day;
> The flying birds two by two return.
> In these things there lies a deep meaning;
> Yet when we would express it, words suddenly fail us.

Despite the cool reception by positivists and scientists, the aesthetic sensibilities of the East are not strangers to the West. Shelley's dwelling on the elusiveness of objects and Wordsworth's passion in nature have expressed the feeling of ineffability with intimacy. So have St. Augustine, Nicolas of Cusa, and other Western mystics. What can be more Taoist than Wordsworth's lines:

> To every natural form, rock, fruits or flower
> Even the loose stones that cover the highway,
> I gage a moral life: I saw them feel,
> Or linked them to some feeling: The great mass
> Lay imbedded in a quickening soul, and all
> That I beheld respired with inward meaning.

One of the most sensitive and recent expressions of no-knowledge in the Occidental literature is given by Eugene O'Neill. In the words of the youngest son, Edmund Tyrone, in *Long Day's Journey Into Night,* the reminiscence flows on:

> When I was on the Squarehead square rigger bound for Buenos Aires. Full moon in the Trades. The old hooker driving 14 knots. I lay on the bowsprit, facing astern, with the water foaming into spume under me. I became drunk with the beauty and singing rhythm of it and for a moment I lost myself—actually lost my life. I dissolved in the sea, became white sails and flying spray, became beauty and rhythm, became moonlight and the ship and the high dim-starred sky. I belonged, without past or future, within peace and unity and a wild joy, within something greater than my own life, or the life of Man, to Life itself! To God, if you want to put it that way.

But how can no-knowledge, which is indescribable and born of silence, be elicited from ourselves? In this respect we should gain some insight into the methodology of learning and inspiration from the East. As Northrup has so well elaborated, there are three conceptual types in the Eastern way of thought. First, there is the concept of the "Differentiated Aesthetic Continuum." This is the initial all-embracing, immediately apprehended totality. The "continuum" emphasizes the all-embracing characteristic; the "differentiated" means that some parts within the continuum are different from others; the "aesthetic" means that there are certain features in the continuum which are qualitatively ineffable. Second, there is the notion of the "Undifferentiated Aesthetic Continuum." This is the continuum component of the parent "Differentiated Aesthetic Continuum" apart from the differentiations. Third, there is the idea of "Differentiations," which are the concrete properties apart from the continuum.

The difference in viewpoint between the East and the West is particularly emphasized in consideration of the concept of the "Undifferentiated Aesthetic Continuum." The idea probably appears untenable to the empirical mind, to which the continuum can but be the total aggregate of the many qualities. The positivism of the West therefore differs from that of the East. The former maintains that the three versions of the East are reducible to the single thought of "Differentiations." The complete meaning is obtained by immediate observations upon atomic objects and properties. It is clear, therefore, that the scientific Westerner would approach a situation by direct and positive assertions and postulations. Things can be theorized about or examined. Nothing need be left undescribed or unsaid.

To the Taoist, there are many observations and sentiments of ineffability. Even in the immediately apprehended, there is the important "Undifferentiated Aesthetic Continuum." It is inconceivable that postulations and positive statements provide us with any contact with such wordless regions of apprehension. As a result of these differences in orientation, the respective methodologies of acquiring knowledge differ significantly between the East and the West. Each has developed techniques especially suitable for the primary interests of its own precincts. The scientific West adopts the positive method and the Taoist East the negative. In the positive method the item under question is intentionally pointed out and described. In the negative method, it is specifically not discussed. By not dissecting the ineffable x in question but merely restricting discourse to objects that it is not, the features of the x are revealed in our dim consciousness.

Many of the parables in the Bible are versions of the negative approach. Even in fields of activity not necessarily close to the church and the book, there is keen appreciation of the indescribability of essences. When the famous American jazz cornettist Louis Armstrong was asked to distinguish his art form from classical music, he replied in typical Buddhist fashion, "If you get to ask, you'll never get to know!"

One may contrast the negative approach in resistance to evil in Christ's "Turn the other cheek" with the positive approach of the older Hebraic "An eye for an eye." We recall the negative challenge that Garibaldi voiced to his men when the defense of Rome appeared hopeless, "Let them who dare to keep fighting the stranger follow me. I give neither pay nor sustenance. I offer only hunger, forced marches, battle and death." We may also compare the positive approach to attaining independence by Washington's fighting army with the negative approach of Gandhi's passive resistance.

Even among executives we notice not infrequent exploitation of negative methods in imparting the art of leadership. Many of the most effective leaders do not use positive tactics in describing the ways of men and the means of their control and direction. Instead, they merely state to their subordinates what is to be done and criticize inept implementing actions. They do not offer apparently or obviously helpful guidance and advice—a practice contrary to all the good books of management. Sooner or later, if the followers are susceptible to inspirations from the province of no-knowledge, they would gain sudden enlightenment on the ineffable principles of human behavior.

Closely tied to this outlook on the development of executives is the selection of the raw material with which to begin. The advice of Confucius along this line goes something like this:

> Refusal to instruct one who is capable of learning entails the waste of a man; instruction of one who is incapable of learning entails the waste of words.

In a similar vein, Chuang-tze tells the story of the Spirit of the Ocean speaking to the Spirit of the River:

> You cannot speak of ocean to a well-frog—the creature of a narrower sphere. You cannot speak of ice to a summer insect—the creature of a season. You cannot speak of Tao to a pedagogue; his scope is too limited. But now that you have emerged from your narrow sphere and have seen the

great ocean, you know your own insignificance and I can speak to you of great principles.

A subtle use of the negative technique in teaching is also illustrated in the Ch'an story: It seems that a certain teacher stuck out his thumb and remained silent whenever he was asked to explain the Tao. His boy attendant would imitate him. One day when this mimicry occurred, the teacher suddenly chopped off the boy's thumb. Whereupon the boy ran away crying. The teacher called out to him. Just as the boy turned, the teacher again stuck out his thumb. Then and there the boy gained sudden enlightenment.

The positive and the negative strategies are not contradictory nor even distinctly separable. They are complementary facets of the one access to total knowledge. As long as we restrict ourselves to the positive, we merely touch the obvious. To tap the secret springs of deep awareness, we must expand into the negative. Because of emphasis on the latter, however, the Orient has never fully developed the positive skills. For this reason the Orient lacked the clear, logical, and methodical empiricism so necessary for material and industrial progress. In its place it has refined the inscrutable smile of the negative.

For ease of presentation the previous pages discussed separately rational knowledge, intuitive knowledge, and no-knowledge. The classification is more didactic than real. Actually they compose an inseparable unity. They may be looked upon as reflections from different angles of the basic quality that makes man man. As in the case of an athlete, one may develop the agility at running, at shooting a sphere through a hoop, at hooking a disc over ice, at parrying a thrust in mid-air. The respective skills are just various forms of expression of the same native "athletic talent." One does not seek different ghosts within the athlete, which are to be allocated to the respective sports. A special training must be selected, however, to sharpen the proficiency in a given direction. The analogy can be extended to rational knowledge, intuitive knowledge, and no-knowledge and the applicable techniques of the positive and the negative. Each of the forms of knowledge is especially effective for certain games in life. Since we are called upon to play the entire series, unlike the athlete who can select only one sport, we should be equipped with the complete spectrum of understanding.

As we look back upon the last six chapters we note that the chief value of science lies in the introduction of a new way of thought. The method relies on postulation, based on rational knowledge. During the past three hundred years this technique has opened up expansive and heretofore inaccessible vistas. But the acquisition of new jewels does not exhaust the treasure troves of old. The wisdom of the sages, amalgamating the elements of intuitive and no-knowledge, remains untarnished. It is still the basic guidance behind the important decisions affecting man as man. Wisdom is the artful way in which rational knowledge, intuitive knowledge, and no-knowledge are mastered, handled, integrated, and applied. Segmented knowledge, as science is wont to offer through its emphasis on rationality, is hardly wisdom. As Cassirer clearly recognized, the "crisis in man's knowledge of himself" today is the fact that "a central power capable of directing all individual efforts ceased to exist." Unfortunately, Cassirer and others have sought this centralizing power within the exclusive nature of man. As can be gathered from the discussions in Chapter 7, in order to penetrate the nature of man, a language beyond the confines of man must be employed. Man cannot know himself through his own knowledge. He must resort to the language of universal scope, that of no-knowledge. This is an important chord for the research executive to remember who is seeking harmony between science and nature.

Chapter 10

The Essential Ferment in Education

OUR TECHNOLOGICAL SOCIETY need not worry about the continued supply of specialists to keep its furnaces burning. The schools are doing an excellent job in providing graduates with this training.

Today's applicants come to organized research with an impressive mass of technical information. However, there seems to be a deficiency somewhere in their arsenal of sensing and feeling. They manifest a skewness which reminds us of Horace's expert coppersmith, "infelicitous at the highest level, because he does not know how to deal with a whole."

In attempting to correct this uneasy state of affairs, many educators in this country allude to the inadequate financial support of the schools. They view with some concern the decreasing ratio of educational to the total expenditure by the United States Government. They point to the adverse trend wherein the ratio of 1 to 2 in 1900 dropped to 1 to 6 in 1950. They are discouraged by the comparisons that between 1940 and 1951, the cost of living index in the United States increased 86 per cent; the hourly wage of industrial workers 138 per cent; the average faculty salary in the universities only 45 per cent. They almost despair at the meager income for public school teachers in 1950, ranging from a low of $1475 to a high of $4500. These figures are contrasted with the minimum wage equivalent of $2500 per year stipulated by the Walsh-

Healy Act that must be paid any worker involved in the production of items to be sold to the Government. They consider it disgraceful that an international philanthropist to the tune of ten billion dollars in 1950 would treat her own teachers with such miserliness.

A heartening appreciation of the fiscal problem is growing. In 1950 the Government subsidized $100,000,000 worth of research in two hundred academic institutions. Although the support is not expected to continue indefinitely at the same level, it did provide a significant stimulation. The National Science Foundation was established in 1950 and was authorized to support academic research up to $15,000,000 per year. Corporations in this country donated $10,000,000 to educational institutions in the same year. Thirty states have now enacted encouraging legislation on corporate gifts. There is a number of foundations organized to contribute to the over-all effort, including the H. J. Heinz Foundation, the National Fund for Medical Education, and the Council for Financial Aid to Education. In 1955 The Ford Foundation distributed $600,000,000 to colleges and hospitals and General Motors gave $4,500,000 to higher education.

Many educators feel that if this trend continues to the point of adequate financial support, attainment of the main goals of education will naturally follow. But this is hardly the complete answer. The wealthier universities themselves seem to be concerned about the same problem of social adjustment among their own graduates. There appears to be a need for a qualitative change in the educational approach itself in a changing world. Let us consider this question as it impinges on science and research.

The deficiency in the newly employed graduate does not seem to affect his first five years of contributions at the bench. It shows itself in naked relief in a position of leadership, beginning with the group supervisor. This shortcoming is the chief reason for by-passing many an otherwise brilliant scientist for advancement into executive positions. It is not the technical knowledge that is lacking; it is the "other."

Inadequacy in technical knowledge can be adjusted without great difficulty. The procedures are well practiced. Deficiency in the "other" is a coat of another color. To impart this "other" knowledge to the employee has always been a main concern of industrial career management programs. One of the chief obstacles hindering its transmission is the indefinable character. Although real, it is as imprecise as an exhilarating spring day. It defies articulate description. It is not dispensed in measured doses. It is absorbed slowly and subconsciously into the moral fiber and intimate intuition of the person over a long period of time. Accordingly, management must look to the shapers of the plastic personality of youth for the major contribution in this process of character-building. Corrective efforts by executives can but be Sysyphean failures, if the incumbent comes firmly cast in an incompatible mold.

Just what is the "other" knowledge? In order to pursue the answer effectively, we must resort to the negative tactics of the East. As the reader recalls from Chapter 9, in the negative approach the specific idea to be put across is never explicitly mentioned. Instead the teacher begins by describing something that is perhaps somewhat like it but which it is not. After "beating around the bush" for a while, the length of which depends upon the skill of the master and the receptivity of the pupil, the latter suddenly gains awareness as to what it is. Presto! There it is. That is all there is to it. We shall therefore discuss vaguely those subjects which altogether may suggest that which they are not. This unmentionable, then, is what the instructors should inculcate in their students over and beyond the technical know-how.

Let us start with the insight into the transcendent totality and, in Eliot's phrase, "the intersection of the timeless with time." All that we call history possesses a future in its heritage. All that we call basic research, applied research, production, business, and morality buttress the totality of our lives. There is no absolute disjunction between the organism and the environment in their continuous interchange of influence and matter. Bare existence is a figment of abstraction. The separation of action from thought is purely a verbal differentiation; in reality there is only unity. Activity is the visible expression of thought, and thought is the invisible stimulus to performance. Life cannot be built along one chain. Knowledge as unadulterated knowledge cannot be integrated into life as pure life. Only life is miscible in life. Frequently the hope is engendered that knowledge and activity can be separately pursued and abstractly developed through many levels of organization and finally integrated as fully matured distinct entities into each other. Such a synthesis cannot be effected; at best it is highly strained. Activity and knowledge must be intimately associated with all other ingredients of life at every focus of nature. [The universe is a single expression.]

The apprehension of the totality is not an intellectual progression in the hermetic conventional sense. It is not taking one factor in the left hand, another in the right hand, shaking them together in the mental test tube to form a product, repeating the process with new additions, ad infinitum. Such an Aristotelian accretive viewpoint hampers our cultural understanding. Nature is not organized in this manner; she is a spontaneous agglomeration. Factual congruity is one with emotional congeniality. Sugars are not added to the liver cells after the organ is fully grown. Neither are pigments added to the flowers after they gain their full shape in the flush of spring. An embryonic leaf of the petunia is just as complete with its potentialities, apparatuses, and diverse structures as the oldest leaf of the giant sequoia.

The discrete additive approach is not unique to inferior technicians of the twentieth century. A hundred years ago Delacroix criticized his contemporary painters for their use of coloration instead of color. By this he meant that color was being added to their figures instead of their figures being created out of color.

The totality and diffusiveness of things are eloquently stated by that Western individualist Emerson in his poem on Brahma:

> If the red slayer thinks he slays,
>   Or if the slain thinks he is slain,
> They know not well the subtle ways
>   I keep, and pass, and turn again.
>
> Far and forgot to me is near;
>   Shadow and sunlight are the same;
> The vanished gods to me appear;
>   And one to me are shame and fame.
>
> They reckon ill who leave me out;
>   When me they fly I am the wings;
> I am the doubter and the doubt,
>   And I the hymn the Brahman sings.

The test of worth of an idea is its relevancy to the stream of life. Masterly utilization of ideas lies in establishing their places in the scheme of the world, in sensing the relative contributions to and dependency upon associated tissues and organs, in recognizing the limitations and capabilities, and in implementing the wisdom of exercising changes in the totality by the judicious manipulation of the proper elements. This exercise keeps knowledge alive and avoids, with Seneca, learning which cures nothing.

The heaping of knowledge needs to be accompanied by a humane polarity. It is the vector quality of learning that determines its social effect. Otherwise, knowledge becomes merely a mass of indeterminate potentialities. Without relevancy, it is an anemic neutrality, that mirage of the pseudosavant, who gauges his own loftiness by his irresponsibility for the fruits of his actions. To be neutral, after all, is merely to be without association. We may know everything about atoms and molecules; we may be masters of the facts of political science; we may be familiar with all the laws governing human relations; we may memorize all the historical sequences of nations. But if such awareness remains unoriented, how shall we shape our lives? A vital question before educators is therefore: Can their system bestow the necessary vector of human-heartedness?

Escape from life fossilizes our thoughts. Our minds become imprisoned in successively more petrified cells. The deadening effect can be seen among some scholastic hermits. They narcissistically contemplate their own brilliance and nod their disdain for the common folks that make the world go 'round—the janitor who removes their trash, the plumber who fixes their sinks, the carpenter who builds their blackboards, the cashier who signs their paychecks, the philanthropist who provides their endowments, the soldier who defends their possessions, the statesman who protects their rights. These scholars should heed the words of the Chāndôgya Upanishad:

> A tied bird, after flying everywhere, settles down, on its perch; the mind, after wandering everywhere, settles down on its life; for, my son! Mind is tied to life.

It is understandable why some scientists separate themselves from the affairs of the world. Like other creative artists the scientist requires a responsive audience. Although he may pursue research chiefly because of an inner personal drive, nevertheless he gains considerable stimulus from the interest, adulation, and pleasure that his work elicits among his associates. A shared emotion is important in his way of life. But when practical people are incapable of appreciating the significance of his work, he begins to seek solace in his own immediate surroundings, retrenching from the common populace. He begins to communicate within an ever-restricting coterie and frown upon his confreres who insist upon maintaining active contact with the lay public and press.

But suppressed attachment is hardly a good reason for detachment. Actually, it is the more educated man who should be more capable than his fellow men in understanding and extending empathy. He should be the one to remember Montaigne's admonition that the worst fatuity is to be "annoyed and exasperated by the fatuities of the world, for it irritates us chiefly with ourselves." Education should confer a sense for the understanding and the communion so necessary for the enrichment of thought. Even Machiavelli, with his notorious reputation for machinations, valued deeply the gracious humanity of man. In one of his letters, written on his estate after he was dismissed from office, we read:

> At nightfall I return home and go to my study and on the doorway take off my rustic garments, stained with mud and mire. I put on my court dress and thus decently reclothed, enter within the ancient courts of ancient men. And there being cordially welcomed with loving kindness, I am fed with the food that alone is my true nourishment, and for which I was born. And here I am not ashamed to hold discourse with them, and inquire the motives of their actions. And they in their humanity reply to me. And so, for the space of four hours I feel no weariness, remember no trouble, no longer fear poverty, no longer dread death; my whole being is absorbed in that of my ancient mentors.

Instead of avoiding ugly reality, scientists should be infused with the zeal of the great artists, like Rembrandt and Shelley. They have gazed directly into the cruelties and sadness of the world and through their talents transformed them into works of richness and joy. Rembrandt's beautiful rendition of a tired laborer and Shelley's conversion of nineteenth century England into a Platonic utopia are eternal inspirations before us. Such greatness requires not only creative ability but a courage of happiness under reality. In this connection there is an old Chinese proverb which goes something like this:

> You cannot stop the birds of sadness from flying over your head, but you can stop them from building nests in your hair.

By seeing life steadily and as a whole, a buffer of wisdom is achieved. There is a tranquillity of mind. Events do not impinge with a singular exaggerated force. This is quite unlike the scientific weighing of matters in isolation. In such an empty scale, a snippet of trouble would bring about a violent swing of the emotions. The ideal we are seeking channels the total force of an event instantly into proper equilibrium within the universe. Only with such an unlimited and frictionless network can a matured perspective, a deep tenderness for all things, and a lasting serenity be maintained under crises and duress.

So much for a negative description of the "other" knowledge. Just how can the educators go about its dissemination? This much is true: The current method of instruction is efficient in imparting rational knowledge. It produces competent ichthyologists, agronomists, horticulturists, aerodynamicists, and the splinter specialists of the day. These talented people bolster our technological society. We cannot do without them. Yet it seems to many apprehensive people that the very dissociation of subjects from each other in our curriculum works against the acquisition of a tender understanding of life. Accordingly, no more popular hue and cry is heard than the advancement of general education. The supporting brief runs along the following vein: Since life consists of many different factors and facets, man should be equipped with a general familiarity with all of them. We should sprinkle his scientific courses with say sociology (since that pertains to the living-togetherness of men), philosophy (since that thinks about thinking), economics (since that makes many of our institutions tick), Graeco-Roman civilization (since many of our ideas come from it), art (since there is a lot around), French (since there are 50,000,000 Frenchmen in the world). With such a background he should be able to recognize these influences in daily living and handle them with greater facility.

The objective behind general education has merit. It provides a taste of many disciplines, which may whet the appetite of the scientist toward a broadening of his limited horizon. But here comes the rub. The poor fellow, having taken hours away from his specialty to undergo the finishing treatment, has not learnt enough science! He cannot make a living in the field for which he had registered. [The many combinations and permutations of curricula over decades of educational experimentation have only repeated the cyclic vogue several times without visibly improving the conjoint art of living and of making a living.]

The educational problem emerges: How can we develop specialists with the "other" knowledge at the same time? Are technical knowledge and the "other" to be taught by mutually exclusive methodologies? Must the humanities and the sciences continually vie for emphasis in the student's curriculum? The thesis presented in this chapter is an optimistic one. There is no need for competition. The procedures are not immiscible. They are not two distinct methods but one simultaneity.

The dangers in modern higher education do not arise from specialization, which is the common whipping boy of educational critics. Specialization is a necessary feature of learning. It provides a penetrating training for the intellect and an inner devotion to the field. The student digs exhaustively to gain a firm hold on the more fundamental roots of knowledge. General education does not elicit these surges from the depths; frequently it is superficial and windblown. We remember Alexander Pope's often-quoted passage:

> A little learning is a dangerous thing;
> Drink deep, or taste not the Pierian spring:
> There shallow draughts intoxicate the brain,
> And drinking largely sobers us again.

Specialization is not the source of social inadequacy. We do not gain the "other" knowledge by eliminating the opportunity for deep appreciation. We must add something to it. Let us seek this essential ferment.

As a prelude there must be a reorientation in some of our general beliefs. Many educators feel that whereas a physical science course like geology gives technical knowledge, a humanities course like sociology provides "other" knowledge. This is not so. With the current organization of teaching, nearly all of the university classes are geared to teach only technical knowledge. The exceptions are due not to the substance or arrangement of the curricula prescribed by deans and department heads but to the genius of the individual professors. Whether or not a course provides technical or "other" knowledge does not depend on the subject matter but on the way it is conducted. Teaching by the positive method, in which things and events are abstracted out of context from the wholeness of nature, can only provide technical knowledge. Treatment of the arts in the "scientific method" merely mimics the mediocre technological courses in divorcing the intellect from the deeper qualities of man. The fact that the bits of data under discussion concern poetry and society instead of gausses and ergs makes them no less a kind of technicism.

The "other" knowledge can be taught only through an adaptation

92

of the negative approach of the East.⌉ As we recall from Chapter 9, in this technique the disciple is tutored without explicit teaching. The subject matter is merely the carrier wave, which conveys the modulated nuances and insights of the "other" knowledge to the subconscious mind of the listener. Utilizing this technique, the lecturer may well teach geophysics with the usual apparatuses and facts. At the same time however, if he has the patience and the skill of the Buddhist Masters, he can excite the germ of enlightenment of the "other" knowledge from the latent potentialities of the pupil. Without extra courses or time he can soak the mentality of the apprentice with suggestiveness. He can develop in the student an awareness of the ineffable sensing and feeling beyond the formulae and equations. The young man learns that the interposing silence between words adds drama to speech and the pauses between notes enhance the vibrancy of music. Guidance to life then becomes the unobstructive evoking of wisdom and beauty between the technical pages and lectures, such as reflected in Benet's couplet:

> You can weigh John Brown's body well enough,
> But how and in what balance weigh John Brown?

A crude sample of the negative approach at teaching can be obtained from the centuries-old sermon of the Zen Master Wu-tzu on sudden enlightenment. He went on to say that it is like learning the art of burglary in the following story: The son of an aging housebreaker decided that it was about time for him to learn the profession to support the family. So he asked his father for lessons. The father approved the proposal and took him along on the next attempt. They broke through a fence, stealthily entered a rich home, and opened a large chest. The father suggested that the son step into the chest and pick out the valuables. Whereupon the son did. As soon as he got in, the father dropped the lid, locked the chest, sneaked out into the courtyard, loudly knocked on the door waking the whole household and quickly retired through the hole in the fence. The excited residents scurried around with their candles and discovered that the thief had gotten away. Meanwhile the son, imprisoned in the chest, was terribly afraid; an idea flashed through his mind. He made a scratching noise like a mouse, at the sound of which the master of the mansion sent the maid to investigate. When the maid unlocked the chest, out jumped the boy, who blew out the candle, pushed the maid aside and ran off with the neighbors on his heels. Passing a well, he lit upon a second thought. He picked up a large stone and dropped it into the well with a loud splash. Hearing the sound the pursuers all gathered around the deep and dark hole, attempting to see the burglar drowning himself. The boy ran on. Safely back at home the youngster blamed the old man for his misfortune. Replied the father understandingly, "Tell me, son, how did you get away?" Whereupon the son recounted the harrowing experience. And the father finally smiled, "There, son, you have now learnt the art of burglary!"

An appreciation of the force of history, for example, can readily be disseminated even in an organic chemistry course. Because of the sheer competition of time it may not be possible to transmit the conventional historical dates and data. But history is charged with motives and their consequences. It is just as practicable to show these factors behind the discovery of the synthesis of ammonia, dyes, pharmaceuticals, and the thousands of chemicals in Beilstein, as it is to delineate the compulsions behind the Macedonian conquest, the Crusades, and the War of 1812. But to imply that scientific activity is free from the human emotions that actually contributed to its very existence and growth is to provide an illusory perspective of the past. It is no wonder that the student fed with such stuff and nonsense cannot leap into the world with adaptive grace.

In the case of art, what is its core if not the intuitive appreciation of the richness, beauty, and infinite shades of human expression? There are more than ample occasions for traversing these essences in a physics experiment, a biological laboratory, an engineering construction, or an isolated observatory. Who can be richer in imagination than the scientist with his concept of the structure of an atom; what more beautiful than histological sections of tissues; what more vivid display of shades than the fireball of an atomic explosion; what deeper emotion of unity than astronomical speculations? Instead, these wonderful opportunities for stimulating a subconscious intimacy of art and science remain largely unexploited by the lecturer. What is usually emphasized in their places are delimited, cold packages of "true-and-false" content.

To be sure, the latter method of instruction is simpler and its preparation less time consuming. When two chemicals are mixed in a vessel, the freshman learns that: X plus Y give A plus B. There are only two products. The reaction is clean-cut. But this is hardly the truth of the "simple" equation. In reality, there are innumerable reactions and inter-actions. The reason why only *A* and *B* are listed instead of *C, D, E,* and a large number of other compounds is the chemist's preoccupation at the moment with *A* and *B*. Had he been more interested in others, he could very well have written the equation: *X* plus *Y* give *C* plus *Z*. The student should be weaned from the idea that there is a single, sharp resultant to a given problem. The well-defined solution is merely man's temporary abstraction out of the totality for expedient and pragmatic attention. It should be more accurately stated thus: *X* plus *Y* give *A* plus *B plus.* It is so with science, with art, with society, with life.

There has been an encouraging trend in the right direction. Take the concept of valencies. As recently as a decade ago, the theory taught was that each atom is endowed with a discrete and integral number of bonds with which it is joinable to the next in forming molecules. Currently it is freely being admitted that valencies do not dance around atoms in nimble retinues of 1, 2, 3, 4, 5, 6. Instead there are the woozy 1.2 bonds, 1.3333 ... bonds, 1.9 bonds, and so on. If such complexities of nature are not shielded from the minds of the pliable and impressionable young-sters, the real world with its multitude of paradoxes will not appear to them as confusing in the future as it has in the past.

The intimate grasp of the intricateness and shadings of life and its consistent expression in action form the basis for tolerance. Unorthodox behavior and thinking on the part of our neighbor will not fill us with horror and disgust. The urge toward his suppression will not arise. His strange ideas are tolerated in the light of the knowledge that complexity and variation are quite natural. There will always be ideologies appar-ently incompatible with each other. If we so wish to eliminate this seeming disharmony of convictions, we will have to destroy all men. But then, the baboon will remain to flaunt his baboonery to the anteater. And if we proceed to destroy all life, the uranium atom with its ninety-two electrons will continue to look askance at the hydrogen atom with its measly one. It is the concept of simplicity and uniformity which is flabby to life. Educational systems that continue to breed ignorant intolerance through the negative instrument of simplified schematic presentations are doing the students no good. They learn the wrong facts; they fall easy prey to undemocratic intolerance and personal perplexity; they forget that every creature has its own proper offerings to God.

Education should also stress factualizing and humanizing of events. Scientists must see themselves as they are. They are just men and women driven by the same temptations, susceptible to the same prejudices, and committing the same errors as the citizens of the pre-science centuries and the laymen of modern times. The annals of science need not be censored and warped to picture scientists as steely paragons of rational virtues. It is not degrading to admit that Copernicus did not have enough data on which to draw valid conclusions, that Kepler relied on the horoscope, that Bacon was frequently mean, that Faraday worked on false theories, that Darwin made lots of mistakes, that Newton was peevish and engaged in petty maneuvers to detract credit from Hooke and Leibniz, that Dickens and Balzac wrote for money or that Sir Robert Walpole and Daniel Webster dealt occasionally in blatant venalities. To recognize these frailties is merely to understand that beneath the scientific and artistic personalities lies the same human protoplasm. Their behavior in private life is not the aspect of their personality which acts on our scientific knowledge through their works. Neither is the perfection of their professional efforts any index of the excellence of their human selves.

Similar discrepancies have also been observed in the stature of nations. Material and physical greatness in a country does not necessarily mean artistic and intellectual greatness. This has been well shown by P. A. Sorokin, A. L. Kroeber, and others. We may recall the glorious creative days of Lessing, Goethe, Schiller, Kant, Mozart, and Beethoven when Germany's national power was but a mere shadow of the Bismarck and Hitler regimes.

In addition to thinking, the student should be provided with the education of feeling. He should not be led into the abject slavery of formal logic and rationality. He should be untethered from the restrictions of verbal and written symbols. He should learn to transcend language, sharing the sensitivities of St. Thomas, who as he wearily put aside his great unfinished treatise, the *Summa Theologica,* said it was "all straw." The Buddhists have always emphasized this wordless communion with nature. This is typified by the following story of a Buddhist Master lecturing to his monks: Just before the sermon began, a bird started singing on a bough outside the monastery walls. The Master kept quiet and everyone listened to the song in attentive silence. As soon as the bird finished, the Master announced that the sermon was completed and departed.

There should be an extension of the student's awareness into the "suchness of nature." The sound of the bell is heard before it rings; the flight of the bird is seen before it flies. If one waits for the bell to be struck before one hears the sound, he is merely listening in the sense world. The latter, of course, is precisely the kind of inelastic knowledge that is stressed using the positive techniques of the day. The striking of the bell brings about its differentiation. What should be sought by the educators in addition and transmitted to the pupils is the sensing of the undifferentiated.

The suchness of nature demands propriety. To develop this point let us use an excerpt of Taoist translations by Lin Yu-tang:

> Those who rely upon the arc, the line, the compass, and the square to make correct forms injure the natural constitution of things. Those who seek to satisfy the mind of man by hampering it with ceremonies and music and affecting humanity and justice have lost the original nature of man. There is an original nature in things. Things in their original nature are curved without the help of arcs, straight without lines, round without compasses, and rectangular without squares; they are joined together without glue and held together without cords. In this manner all things grow with abundant life, without knowing how they do so. They all have a place in the scheme of things and . . . [the scheme] may not be tampered with. Why should then the doctrines of humanity and justice continue to remain like so much glue or cords, in the domain of the Tao to give rise to confusion and doubt among mankind? . . . He who would be the ultimate guide of the world should take care to preserve the original nature of man. Therefore, with him the original is not like joined toes, the separated is not like extra fingers, what is long is not considered excess, and what is short is not regarded as wanting. For a duck's legs, though short, cannot be lengthened without dismay to the duck, and a crane's legs, though long, cannot be shortened without misery to the crane. That which is long in nature must not be cut off, and that which is short in nature must not be lengthened.

Even wisdom, sincerity, and virtue may interfere with the suchness of nature. Chuang-tze describes a pertinent situation as follows:

> With the truly wise, wisdom is a curse, sincerity like glue, virtue only a means to acquire and skill nothing more than a commercial capability. For the truly wise make no plans and therefore require no wisdom. They do not split apart and therefore require no glue. They do not want anything and therefore need no virtue. They sell nothing and therefore are not in want of a commercial capability.

97

It is this glimpse into the suchness of phenomena that unfolds an estimate of the results before the experimentation, an account of the profits before the sales, a vision of the aftermath before the war. It provides a realization of the consequences before the act, a reverberation of the echo before the shouting. It elicits a sense of destiny, a feeling of the future. There is nothing mysterious about this in principle. We constantly apply it in an infinitesimal way. We buy a steak at the grocer's looking forward to a savory platter. We board a bus expecting arrival at the office. We sense the tension of the day before we set foot in the office. America's greatest poetess of the nineteenth century, Emily Dickinson, has remarkably put it:

> I never saw a moor,
> I never saw the sea;
> Yet know I how the heather looks,
> And what a wave must be.

All men are born with potentialities in this direction. It is a function of education to make them kinetic in their lives.

Unfortunately, simplification and standardization are creeping into the habits of American teaching. Clarity of presentation is considered a prime virtue in the selection of textbooks. The more readily it enables one to memorize data to square with questions in anticipated examinations, the higher the manual is held in esteem. Conversely, quizzes are geared to the format and outlines of the chapters. Adventitious matter and circuitous dark passages are deleted. Schematic diagrams galore.

It is frequently overlooked that some of the most difficult texts from which to teach (rational knowledge) may be the most effective with which to impart, through the negative method, the essence of the humanities. Clarity of presentation should be extended beyond the explicit teachings of rational knowledge to the ineffable features of nature. Fuzziness in the explicit may be the threshold of lucidity in the ineffable. The wisdom of the teacher lies in their proper blending.

The view presented in these paragraphs does not support the light-hearted fashion in which personal relations between students and professors are regarded in some departments. Some of the so-called advanced and progressive institutions have even made class attendance optional. The student is required only to pass examinations. Contacts with the teacher are considered crutches for lagging pupils. We can look at two of the presuppositions underlying such unimaginative instruction. The first is the assumption that imparting facts and rational techniques alone constitutes the aim of education. The second is that while imparting the "other" knowledge may be desirable, the professor himself is unable to pass it along in his technical lectures. He should accordingly be contented with facts and logic which, if the student is sufficiently gifted, can very well be learnt without any outside assistance. Either premise, if adopted, would deprive the students of the rich enlightenment of intuitive knowledge and no-knowledge. In order to impart this essential guide to wholesome living, the contagious contact between the student and the professor would appear to be mandatory.

What is essential in education is a receptiveness to intuitive extrapolations into the totality of nature and a communion with her in the realm of no-knowledge. This is a lasting outlet for the scientist to stray beyond his own mental groove of professionalism and specialism to the open plains of life. Implementing techniques of transferring this superrational knowledge must be devised. The fashionable abstract and positive approach seems inadequate. It should be extended to include the matured negative skill of the Zen Masters. Through this means many people in the Orient have gained a discernment which leads to tranquillity and wisdom. There may be something in it that the professors of science can profitably assimilate.

Part IV

Management
and
Practice
of
Modern
Science
and
Research

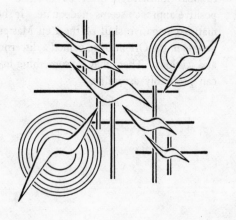

Chapter 11

Freedom in Organized Research

BEGINNING WITH THE MIDDLE of the nineteenth century there was a gradual diminution of unbounded free enterprise. Before that time the advance of personal liberty had been the driving force behind two centuries of impressive progress. The subsequent entrenchment of modern industrialism caused the rapid decay of rugged individualism. So far as sheer license is concerned, writers are quick to point out that there was more in London during the reign of Charles I in the early seventeenth century than there is in any industrial metropolis in the world today.

Take the Republican millionaire in Chicago in 1944. He is boxed in on all sides. Two thirds of his income go to a government dominated by a party he has been trying for a decade to defeat. The very idea of Franklin Delano Roosevelt as his president nauseates him. His investments are regularly and strictly scrutinized. He cannot say what he pleases in his advertisements. He cannot undercut his competitors by whatever means at his disposal. He cannot obtain raw materials for his plants except such as are rationed to him by a board of strangers. He cannot deal with workers save within a procedure prescribed by a group of people in Washington six hundred miles away. He cannot send materials through the mail, save those approved by postal regulations.

He talks about free enterprise with nostalgic enthusiasm. And deep down inside, he confesses that ranging freedom is a thing of the past.

With such diminishing independence, we should recast our perspective against the background of the industrial age. We can no longer expect the symbolic relics of the freedom of surging romanticism to fit into the trappings of its destroyer. We should, therefore, review the concept of freedom as it applies to organized research, which is one of the distinctive aspects of the modern industrial economy. This is the purpose of the chapter.

In the eyes of the scientist, there is hardly a more appealing condition in an organization than freedom. Untrammeled expression has always been a goal of creative artists. The glorification of the free self in Ibsen's drama, the vitalistic concepts in Bergson's philosophical dissertations, the life-force in Shaw's writings are all expressions of the deeply felt solidarity.

Freedom is usually described in terms of the absence of restraints. Our most cherished liberties have been treated in this absentee fashion in the Bill of Rights. To the modern researcher anything that inhibits freedom is considered wrong in principle. Measured managerial intervention is acceptable only as a necessary evil. We need not dwell on this well-known sentiment except to admit its invasive forcefulness. It may be respected, used, sublimated, channeled, or crushed—but not ignored.

By its very title, organized research appears to come into direct confrontation with freedom of research. Assembling a team and merging diverse personalities into a harmonious unit constitute a progressive pinching on the latitude of the individual. There is a submergence of singular identity.

To some extent the change in the degree of individuality as one goes from an independent type of research to an organized type can be compared to the difference between sculpture and architecture. Sculpture is usually the work of single creators. Each piece of work is linked to one sculptor. He alone determines the medium, lines, and modes; he need not compromise his visions and chisels in a cooperative manner with others. Such is not the good fortune of architects. Architecture is more of a social art. The architect must adjust his plans to the implementing capabilities of the artisans and laborers. His talent, as well as that of each of the thousands of individual contributors, is assimilated in the immensity of the project.

Many attempts have been made toward fitting the concept of freedom into the confines of an organized structure. Compromisers propose that the secret lies in not "over organizing" but striking the optimal ratio of unhindered action on the part of the scientist and control on the part of the executive. Contract theorists point to an exchange of rights on the part of the citizen for protection and general welfare furnished by the state. Others claim that knowledge rather than will is the important consideration. An ass is a slave so long as it does not recognize the necessity of a load and chafes under it rather than willingly shoulders it. Some directors follow the principle that one has freedom when he *thinks* he has. They manage to keep the staff satisfied by direction through subtle indirection. Finally, there are the endless discussions over such metaphysical alternatives as freedom versus determinism and freedom as self assertion versus freedom as derived from God.

It is not a simple matter to focus clearly on these points of view. Freedom seems to be a shifting notion. Souls of nobility are lifted to their loftiest heights in their battle for freedom. For knaves it remains a chameleon camouflage for unobstructed poltroonery and ulterior selfishness. Even among the well-intentioned, the parameters vary. To Jean Jacques Rousseau freedom is emotional expression; to Roger Williams it is religious liberty; to William Lloyd Garrison it is emancipation of the Negro; to Henry David Thoreau it is absence of coercion; to David Ricardo it is industrial liberty; to Eugene Debs it is economic equality.

Let us analyze the term freedom of research. The scientist cannot achieve independence by abandoning the world. He can only express his individualism in the midst of it. Birth and death, rain and sunshine, custom and religion, history and will—all set the scene and walls of his intellectual playground. The concept of freedom without boundaries is an illusion. The poet is bound by the meter, the dancer by the rhythm, the painter by the pigments, the judge by the written word.

In an expansive Sahara we are not free; we are only lost. The dilemma in which worshippers of absolute freedom find themselves has been depicted by many writers. Kierkegaard labored long on the poor soul overwhelmed by doubts, loneliness, and insignificance. There is no point of reference with which his power can be guided. In Kafka's

The Castle we read of the complete lifelong failure of the helpless man frantically trying to find the mysterious inhabitants of the place to counsel him as to his part in the scheme of things. Total freedom, it turns out, is an awesome void.

To say that a scientist is free to take electron photomicrographs without the availability of an electron microscope is to jest with words. To say that a research fellow is free to attend a scientific meeting without providing the necessary travel funds is a mere vaunting of generalities without specific implementation. Free choice for the researcher is at the very outset circumscribed by earthy finances.

Even if money is available, there are other insuperable limitations to his desires. Clearly a scientist is not unobstructed in his fancies to work on any subject whatsoever. His life span may be too short to develop the chromosome map of elephants, for example. His limited imagination, insight, or knowledge may prevent him from properly framing the necessary presuppositions or experimental attack on intriguing problems. Can the brilliant geneticist Thomas Hunt Morgan work in seismological fields? Or the brilliant physicist Niels Bohr on yeast taxonomy? The contemporary state of the art itself may not be ripe for the desired study. Would there have been an Einstein had there not been a Newton and a Planck to compost the soil on which his relativity blossomed? It is apparent that researchers are not, to quote H. Butterfield, "autonomous godlike creatures acting in a world of unconditioned freedom."

There is also a peculiar self-imposed serfdom, which has become a sort of competitive cult in recent times. The blackmailing of intellectual freedom by expensive, specialized, fixed installations is one of the dangers of the current financial plenty for research. Not too infrequently an apparatus of considerable cost is built to carry out certain unusual measurements, only to doom the servile scientists to a life of repetitive measurements. Soon the machine assumes the directorship of research. No longer is the mind of the researcher the determinant of experimental plans. Concern for the capability of the equipment becomes the overriding consideration. The more exorbitant the price, the higher the ransom. When the value exceeds a million dollars the mental slavery may run into generations. It takes rare courage to junk the facility after it has served the human purpose for which it was originally built. It is often easier to drivel along in a litany to the mechanical idol. [It is a puzzle of the times that scientists so outspoken against thought control by other men would so unwittingly embrace thought control by money and machines.]

Throughout the centuries from feudalism to industrialism, from scholasticism to romanticism to technicism, the concept of freedom has been expressed in various ways: The Lockean freedom of conscience to believe, the German freedom of will to do, the Anglo-American political freedom to vote, the Marxist economic freedom from capital, the Latin and Spanish psychological freedom of the emotions and sentiments, and the four freedoms of the Atlantic Charter. These different forms of freedoms are actually abstractions. As discussed in earlier chapters, abstractions are always exaggerated emphases. The actuality should be grasped in its totality. When considered in this fashion all of these freedoms and their ancillary anxieties can be subsumed under a single whole. This is the freedom of growth.

[The freedom of growth is a basic, inexorable drive in all living creatures.] From the earliest glimmerings of life, the protean amoeba, the wriggling worm, and the Neanderthal man—all were under the compulsion to grow. [It is not the competition for Darwinian survival that governs the actions of the biological world; it is the struggle for growth.] Were it simply a matter of mere existence, plants would not spread their roots in the jungle far and beyond the ready minimum. Parasitic vines would not entwine their tendrils greedily and graspingly. Animals would not devour voraciously. Only the urge of growth, pushing plants and animals toward ever-expanding boundaries and ever-increasing numbers, can account for such luxuriance in the wilds of nature.

In the human race the concept of survival does not explain the insatiable demands for progress. If it were a matter of mere living, man would be content to sit. But the very idea of growth implies "more." [Existence is only a means to the end of growth.] It is for this reason that most men are basically incapable of satisfaction, or to put it more graciously, are progressive. [It is the slope of the curve rather than the absolute value that is the compelling index of desire.] Herein lies the obsession of professors to become deans, of Nichol medalists to become Nobel laureates, of contenders to become champions, of millionaires to become multimillionaires, of national leaders to become international statesmen. Labor unions do not strike for living wages; they strike for growing wages. Industrialists are not seeking a surviving income for their corporations; they are striving for a growing income. Security lies not in the assurance of life, but in the guaranty of growth.

"Grow or die" is almost axiomatic with business. Particular attention is given to flexibility and adaptability in large companies to meet challenging and changing economic environments. The maintenance of a liquid condition is a springboard for growth. The hedging against recessions and depressions, the buffeting against seasonal and cyclical trends in customer demands, the providing of new avenues of development, the introduction of diversification are all derivatives of plans for insured growth. Even income is at times sacrificed for the firm's growth. In the long run, continued growth is the most effective way toward enlarged profits.

The same quest for growth is the central problem of international peace. How can a country raise its own standard of living without suppressing that of another? It is not a matter of coexistence that is plaguing the world but the struggle for co-growth.

The intimate relationship between a satisfying life and growth was extolled five decades ago by John Butler Yeats thus: "Happiness is neither virtue nor pleasure nor this thing nor that but simply growth. We are happy when we are growing."

Scientists, too, want to grow physically, intellectually, and spiritually. To fulfill this development in time, this process of perfecting, they must have the attendant freedom. This is the freedom in reality for which the scientist has been groping in his search for the so-called freedom of research.

With this clarification before us the problem of freedom in organized research begins to look more hopeful. We need not share the pessimism of Einstein, who reminisced in 1954 that were he young again, he would be a plumber rather than a scientist in order to enjoy that "modicum of freedom still available in modern society." Organized research is not necessarily exclusive of freedom. There needs to be only a shaping of conditions conducive to the growth of its scientists; these conditions may be grouped under physiological headings of favorable physical conditions, resupply of nutrients, sufficient room for growth, symbiosis, extensive range, and individual specificity.

There is a common feeling that what an institution needs first of all is a stimulating leader. The towering giant can then sprinkle his knowledge and imagination all over the lot, causing beautiful thoughts and valuable inventions to spring forth. The contributions of an inspiring leader are obviously important, and it may well be that no organization can be great without a great director. But one overpowering oak does not a garden make. The vitality of the group cannot be built on this one dominating personality. It requires growth in the broad base of its staff.

Not much need be said about the familiar requirement of a fertile environment. There must be encouraging conditions of purely elemental factors, such as, salaries, equipment, sympathetic management, and the general amenities with which every gentleman is familiar.

Resupply of nutrients is an obvious requirement. For scientists, sources of continued replenishment of ideas and knowledge include the literature and opportunities to meet with conferees. For this reason management should consider requests to maintain adequate library facilities, to attend technical meetings, and to sponsor scientific symposia in a sympathetic light. These cannot be treated as added frills or recoverable expenditures in times of economy. They are fundamental cravings from the very deep and natural desire for growth. They must be met to nourish a living laboratory.

That there must be room for growth is without question. Personality cannot blossom in slavery. In this regard special pains need to be taken by pyramidal organizations. Supervisory positions and scientific standing should not be regarded as synonymous. Promotion along the managerial echelons should not be looked upon necessarily as the only index of acceptable growth. Scientific stature can be enhanced without any change in one's relative location in the hierarchy. Unfortunately the chart-bound mentality of many a laboratory refuses to recognize this avenue of growth. By its failure to provide appropriate financial recognition, it has induced a frustration in the mind of many a brilliant scientist, and a symbolic lid has been clamped upon his development. A similar ceiling is imposed when a supervisor of less-matured qualities is placed over him. It is important in those cases where this is necessary that administrative capability not be confused with scientific competence and proper regard be paid in recognition of the continued growth of both parties.

Symbiosis is common in nature. Frequently two species of organisms are found producing jointly a result which neither is able to approach alone. Algae and fungi, for example, live symbiotically as lichens. There are thousands of other groupings, the members of which stimulate each other's development. The availability of this advantage is one of the inherent characteristics of organized research with its varied scientific disciplines and skills in the same sociological unit. William Allen White described the intangible cross-fertilization of spiritual goodness in group effort:

> Let strong men be mean. Let weaklings be lazy and envious. Let the mediocre man be complacently befuddled. So it has always been. Put them to work side by side—the grasping, the do-less, the bewildered. A hidden grace in each of them—perhaps tolerance or a shamefaced nobility or maybe an innate sense of fairness—amalgamates their baser qualities. A pattern of social conduct emerges, strange and full of friendly purpose. They who seem to be pulling and hauling, jostling and clamoring, have done a day's work that is somehow good. But they only are as competent and wise as they are free. So the wisdom of kindness—let us call it the love of man—comes to bless their labor.

Another freedom that can be realized only in group effort—a soccer team, a family, a research laboratory—is the wider latitude of error of the individual. There is always the covering of each other's mistakes, the retrieving of each other's losses, and the compensating for each other's weaknesses among the members of the unit.

But the greatest benefit of organized research as a contributor to the growth of scientists has been passed over entirely too lightly. This is the extension of the range of effectiveness of their thinking and effort to the public domain. It is the enlargement of their participation in power, which according to Cicero is the essence of freedom itself. In many cases organized research is the only means by which freedom in action can be experienced by a researcher. The force of a technically continuous organization provides the momentum to the initial concept of a scientist through fruition in social good. By this means his ideas gain positive freedom in their realization; his humanitarian desires acquire liberating expression in their fulfillment. To give concrete forms and aesthetic body to his thoughts is to free them from the prisons of buried publications into the free and active state of human welfare. Only in this manner can the freedom for completed growth be attained and ideas lend their power to the meaning of life.

In the formulation of administrative regulations, management should observe the simple phenomenon that plants and animals require different environments and nutrients. It should be wary of general schemes of management in overweaning individuals to blind group orthodoxy. Growth is not the reduction of everyone to the same pattern. The growing isodiametrical cells in a vigorous embryo soon differentiate into many types: bone cells, freely migrating phagocytes, striated muscle cells, nerve fibers, glandular cells. Growth is not only a matter of size; it also involves the florescence of the individual endowments to their full capacity and tonus. So it is with a laboratory of scientists. The feeling of freedom is an individualized affair; each scientist must personally be made to sense the freedom of growth. To be sure, there are common factors, but to develop the full richness of growth of the individuals requires selective treatment. It is for this reason that flexible rather than rigid rules are most appropriate for the management of research.

There are considerable variations in self-interest among professional people. The businessman is quite different from the physician and the scientist. Whereas advertising, credit risk, and price competition are normative guides of common acceptance with the businessman, they are not entertained by the physician in his ministration to the sick. While ghost-writing is accepted as common practice by men in hierarchical organizations, the credit of authorship is one of the most jealously guarded commodities among scientists.

Even among factory employees, where the subtle intellectual variations are not as sharply drawn, Elton Mayo has shown experimentally that the mental disposition of workers to the individualized atmosphere is the principal factor behind increased production. The details of supervision or working conditions were less influential. Frequently the mental reaction carried over from home problems was the controlling factor.

There is a subtle danger involved in overemphasizing the uniformity of managerial treatment of creative activities. It is the breakdown in integrity among members of the research team. An inherent frailty in some people is covetousness of the virtues, riches, fame, and talents of others. In mild form, the feeling expresses itself in a mimicry of the envied. People are driven toward imitating the mannerisms, adopting the style, and cultivating the habits of that paragon, who might well have lived in another age under alien conditions. Their individualities are being forced into an imaginary incompatible prototype. The possibility does not enter their envious minds that had the good Lord intended the transmigration of individualities, He would have made the switch Himself. And who knows but that even greater talents and wealth are hidden within their own chests of fate, if only they would pause and examine their stores. [To cultivate the self to the fullest perfection of one's nature is the sincerest expression of integrity.] But to chisel one's life after another's is but an act of cheap counterfeiting. Management must take care not to aggravate the temptation. To enforce strictly a uniform set of rules, regulations, and patterns of behavior is to elevate an abstract norm for the individuals to emulate. The bridge of transition joining this state with the breakdown of integrity is only a short span.

Actually, as Dean John Burchard has reminded me, "It is the nature of the chains and not their mere existence that determines what limitations there are on creativity." He pointed out that the Council of Nicaea in the eighth century set down a series of guidelines which could be interpreted as iconographic statements on cathedrals, within which the artist had to live. Yet the good work of the medieval painters and sculptors was not sterilized by these conceptual restraints.

The excommunicated life in a dingy garret did not inhibit Spinoza from creating one of the greatest philosophical systems of all time. Paul Gauguin's depressed state of mind did not stand in the way of his capturing the Tahitian beauty on his vivid canvases. The severe physical discomforts of chronic asthma accompanied by high fevers and rheums which forced Marcel Proust to spend much of his life in bed with sweaters, mufflers, gloves, stockings, nightcaps, and long nightgowns did not prevent him from composing his brilliant masterpiece, *Remembrance of Things Past*. The nonacademic environment of a patent office did not discourage Einstein from his revolutionary thoughts in physics. [Absolute freedom therefore is not a sine qua non to self-realization and growth.]

Fostering conditions for growth presupposes the existence of a capacity for growth. The great freedom for growth is ultimately realized in a properly managed organized research effort through a reciprocal stimulation of these two responses. It is in the vigorous participation in this freedom that the researcher finds the outlet for his scientific creativeness. It is in the artistic nurturing of this freedom that the executive finds the source for his moral creativeness.

Chapter 12

Values and Incentives in Organized Research

WESTERN THOUGHT HAS ALWAYS STRESSED VALUES. Its philosophical and theological systems of thousands of years are charged with value concepts. When science entered the scene and threw down her challenge, the question arose as to the fate of these values. Various schools of explanation developed. The humanists attempted to demonstrate the separation of values from metaphysics. Regardless of how we conceive the world, our emotional intuition is supposed to operate independently and tell us what the values are. But the results are not altogether convincing. Other thinkers had maintained that our moral values cannot be reconciled with the evolutionary doctrine of Darwin and suggested a revolutionary change in the governing theses. The squaring of science with values became a major philosophical problem of the day. The most brilliant minds have been and are still wrestling with this formidable question. While their resolution is pending, it may be well for us to gather some of the essential aspects of these dissertations and fit them into the management of organized research.

Values are roughly divided into two types: instrumental and intrinsic. Instrumental values lie in the means to something else. Money is a good illustration. It is a means to power, fame, and happiness. Intrinsic values are those desired for themselves. Tradition has long followed the three intrinsic values of goodness, truth, and beauty. All others are considered instrumental. To be sure, the average man on the street would be hard put to choose between happiness and any one of the three. But these three, the philosopher tells us, are what the people ought to seek.

The question immediately arises whether or not judgments of goodness, truth, and beauty are subjective or objective. A Chinese saying goes: "Hsi Shih was a beautiful woman, but when her features were reflected in the water, the fish were frightened away." If value judgments are merely subjective, then all arguments about them are meaningless. This is the disconcerting wall separating the irreconcilable objective and subjective schools. They are no closer to agreement today than they were two thousand years ago.

To have objective ultimate goodness, truth, and beauty, we must have absolute standards. The realization of these standards is difficult, considering the many religions and moral codes, the large number of lawyers, and the wide assortment of stuff peddled as art. The crucial question is: Who is to decide?

Some say judgments of value should be made relative to the individual. The extreme position is propounded by the atheistic existentialism of Jean Paul Sartre, that man is "condemned to be free." Each person is his own judge. Dewey proposes society as the criterion. He joins theory with action. Solutions should be sought for problems that retard the community. Those that help have value; those that don't do not. Other thinkers suggest that moral values are relative to the needs of the state or the ruling class.

Positivistic enthusiasts question the very idea of value itself. Upon an analysis of language the logical positivists insist that so-called judgments of values are really not judgments at all. They are only statements of feelings and emotions, which are excluded entirely from theoretical formulation. The objective validity of a norm can neither be verified empirically nor deduced from empirical propositions.

A less radical theory of value comes from the neopositivist Kraft. He showed that most normative concepts also possess a descriptive content. The descriptive content is what is specified in the value terms. "Morally good," for example, is defined as conformity to a moral law. "Beautiful" is given as agreement to a harmonious organization of parts within a pleasing whole. Such an outline provides a basis for factual and theoretical analysis of values and norms. One value judgment can be determined to be consistent with another; a more general value judgment can be broken down into logical subsumed judgments; one value can be deduced from another.

The attitude toward the defined theoretical substance forms the basis for the specific normative judgment of say, what is "good" or "beautiful." Value judgments are meaningful from the standpoint of not only the speaker but also the listener. There is a certain degree of sharing through persuasion. Hypothetically, there is a chance for universal concurrence. Values that have acquired the status of the "absolute" are nothing more than those which have been accepted as a matter of course in a given community. Specific value judgments can then be dissected objectively once the universally accepted norms are presupposed as fundamental. Thus, there can be a conditional logical inquiry into value. There can be no unconditional assertions of absolute values.

There is also the view that things are desirable because they have value and not vice versa. Values are absolute and not relative. The definitive point of view leads directly to the measure of objectivity. Many thinkers assume that values follow directly from God. Others consider values absolute only as the terminal worth toward which the universe is evolving. The affirmations of objective values presuppose an intuition which is capable of gaining insights into the ultimates. But our certainty stops short of this frontier.

On a more practical level Adam Smith distinguished value in use from value in exchange. The former is found in anything that fulfills a human need. A thing has value in exchange in relation to other commodities. Other theorists prefer restricting value to the latter class and utility to the former. Much thought has been given to the conversion factor in exchange values. In bartering a Renoir canvas for litchi nuts, what should be the conversion factor for trade?

The Marxists and the Anglo-Americans have arrived at different answers with the Marxists concluding that what goods have in common is the output of human labor that went into their making. Individual preference has little direct relationship to worth, nor is the price the aggregate effect of all individual preferences. Value is not set by the demands.

Values and Incentives in Organized Research

Most Anglo-Americans favor the psychological theory of value. This states that economic goods can be negotiated on the basis of what is introspectively and psychologically wanted. The price varies with the demand. Jevons feels intrinsic value does not exist. Value is not a thing; nor does it reside in a thing. There may be properties inherent in a substance like gold which may affect its value. But the word value merely expresses the circumstances of its exchange for another item in a certain ratio. The ratio is influenced by the wants of the people which are based on pleasure and scarcity.

The Jevons theory of value concerns the economic field. It defines neither ethical nor political values. The United States New Deal in the nineteen thirties and forties used economics as an instrument for political values. The question was not whether or not the decisions were economically sound. The important consideration was how the political or ethical good, such as social well-being, improved labor conditions, and assured employment, could be implemented in the most economical fashion. The business booms and depressions were accordingly reduced by compensating government taxation, spending, control of interest, and other fiscal policies. This planning was largely influenced by Keynes' thinking.

Whether or not the Keynesian theory maintained the political values which were sought need not be considered in this book. More appropriate discussions can be readily found in the political and economic literature. It is briefly introduced to stress the extreme care that must be exercised in the distinction of various kinds of values, which are at the same time intermixed. Value as an end is different from value as a means to another value as an end.

The confusion of ends and means has generated a strange twist in government research in this country over the last decade. For some reason the aphorism, two heads are better than one, has become assiduously worshipped in certain temples of planning. Great emphasis is being paid to extensive discussions in conferences. The selection of channels of investigation is made by vote in many instances. Dozens of consultants and advisers must consider a proposal before action can be initiated. The greater the number of petitioners to a project, the more worthwhile it is taken to be.

Such an advisory system may be said to have something in its favor.

Advisers are not hampered by operational routine in their analysis of the situation. They provide the fresh and detached antidote for mental staleness. They are objective and free from suspicion of favoritism. Their importance was recognized thousands of years ago in the old Indian Panchatantra stories, in which we find the admonition: Better have as king a vulture advised by swans than a swan advised by vultures.

It is unfortunate, however, that overemphasis on consultation and coordination has led to a confounding of values at different levels and of values as a means and as an end. The expertness of an individual in a particular science frequently overflowed into decisions influencing the purposes for which the discipline was but the means. For example, the value of an army lies in its capability to defend the nation. Research and scientific practices within the agency are tools for the accomplishment of its purpose. The value of these instruments stems from their suitability as means, not as ends. Whether or not they lead to a higher standard of theoretical science per se in the military structure is not the primary criterion of value. The fundamental question must be faced: Will they enhance the military's worth as a defender of the country? The management techniques must be fashioned accordingly. The abstract quality of scientific worth is superseded by the power of the military might in this instance, just as the enjoyment of a picture involves a higher grade of value than that of a component color.

The same analogy can be made for industrial concerns and their laboratories and for universities and their research groups. Each parent institution has its distinctive mission.

Clearly, then, the use of advisers, expert in particulars and means but not intimately aware of the totality of the prime objectives, requires delicate judgment. Skill must be exercised in the selection of advisory panels and management consultants, in the direction of suitable questions, and in the implementation of the proposals. We should beware of such confounded questions as: Should an industrial laboratory adopt the academic point of view with regard to fundamental research? Should universities be businesslike? One finds such topics debated in fashionable and learned symposia. Actually, the guidance of any institution should be developed in the light of its own goals. It should not, without careful scrutiny, adopt the means peculiar to other agencies, which are geared to a distinctly different end.

There is another managerial area in which a need exists for clear distinction between ends and means. As an outcome of the pressure against unnecessary duplication of effort in the Government, a feeling has been generated among some of the staff planners that there must be not only a single assignment of ends but also a single assignment of means. An agency may be given the responsibility for certain functional missions. But if it feels that the conduct of say basic research is required, it is discouraged from conducting investigations in those scientific disciplines which have been allocated to another agency. This distribution of monopolies of means implies a fogginess of insight. Assignment should be restricted to ends. Tampering with the free use of scientific disciplines as means to authorized ends results from a self-injuring confusion in the management of research.

In the *Lü Shih Ch'un Ch'iu,* a compendium of philosophical writings in the third century B. C., a contrast was made between people engaged in the "root" and those in the "branch" occupations. Farmers were ascribed to the root group; in times of crises they could not carry their valuables with them. As a consequence they remained and defended the land. Members of the branch class, such as merchants, had more easily transportable properties. There was accordingly a greater temptation for the branch people to abandon the country in danger. For this reason, agriculture was looked upon with warmer favor than commerce.

The comparison no longer holds for modern society. Two thousand years have made considerable changes in the texture of life. Nevertheless, a mite of learning can be gleaned from this ancient sentiment by directors of research.

Of the various occupations the intellectual and the scientific professions possess the most private and the most readily transportable assets—their knowledge and personal ability. According to the *Lü Shih Ch'un Ch'iu,* other things being equal, such persons would appear less attached to any particular clan or institution. They can afford to be nomadic.

The task of the executive is to analyze the instrumental and intrinsic values which exist in the minds of scientists and to provide nourishing environments in the research institution so that they can root deeply. It is not merely a question of interposing deterrents, such as the forfeit of pensions, seniority rights, and residual bonuses to preclude the loss of one's staff to competing laboratories. There is no net gain to the creative community from such inhibitions. As a matter of fact, a few changes in employment in the course of one's career may prove profitable both to the individual and the organization. The outlook of the scientist is broadened and the exchange brings about a cross-fertilization of ideas. In any case, the important philosophic challenge before the executive is: How can organized research be changed from a branchlike to a rootlike occupation? How can the concepts of value for the scientist be fitted into those of organized research, so that he will exhibit the same attachment to his laboratory as the farmer to his land?

There is no particular profit for us to belabor the well-worn incentives that splash over the employment advertisements every day: lucrative salaries, high pensions, favorable sick benefits, insurance, interesting work, friendly associates, wonderful opportunities for advancement. Nor is it necessary to inquire into the usual conditions about which an applicant asks: freedom of research, publication of findings, attendance at scientific meetings, and relief from the bugbear of administrative red tape. These topics have been digested in other texts and have been touched upon in Chapter 11. Attention will be focused here on the aesthetic and philosophical overtones.

The most tenacious sentiment that the peasant shows over his land is the feeling of "home." He is familiar with it, friendly to it, part of it. This enthusiasm is frequently not felt by many researchers for their organized laboratories. Current circumstances make it difficult. First of all, the average young scientist enters the outer world with seven years of negative indoctrination against the more purposeful nature of intellectual challenge in organized research. He says goodbye to his classmates, who choose to remain in the universities, in an apologetic air for "selling his research soul" for a paltry salary differential of two hundred dollars a month. Many of the scientists never get over their basic longing for the free academic pastures; the organized ranch will always be an orphanage to them. The research manager must dissolve the aesthetic prejudices the young researcher brings with him and convert him into a team player. This is the first step toward making the new associate feel at home.

The next step is to increase his familiarity with and his personal attachment to what he is doing. This will provide a stabilizing force which can become a main strut for a satisfying livelihood. A simple contributing practice of some of the more enlightened laboratories may be given as an illustration. It is permitting the scientist a certain privilege of selecting from proposed research problems. Under such an arrangement he will always be treading friendly paths. Furthermore, his personal end-value sought in the solution of the chosen study chimes with that of the institution itself. Rather than impose problems on intellectually unconvinced and reluctant though otherwise cooperative scientists, the better routine in the long run would be a shift in personnel.

The third step is to insure a promise of satisfaction. It is important that this psychic compensation be clear and convincing. In this respect the scientist is no different from other human beings. Man must be made to feel that his work will lead to some good and usefulness. Even Egyptian artisans during the days of the pyramids had walked off their jobs because of a belief that the bricks they had been ordered to produce would not show a high quality because of the absence of straw. Dostoievski described the same dread in his *House of the Dead.*

> If it were desired to reduce a man to nothing—to punish him atrociously, to crush him in such a manner that the most hardened murderer would tremble before such punishment—it would be necessary only to give his work a character of complete uselessness . . . Let him be constrained to pour water from one vessel to another, or to carry earth from one place to another and back again, then I am persuaded that at the end of a few days the prisoner would strangle himself or commit a thousand crimes punishable with death, rather than live in such an abject condition and endure such torments.

Finally, there is the genuine desire of engaging a scientist with all intentions of permanence. No quicker way is there of dampening enthusiasm and love than "fair weather friendships." The cyclic support of research, drastically changing in tune with the ebb and flow of taxation and profits, is shortsightedness. In the first place, there is a recurrent loss of know-how, which has been built up by the company over a period of years. In effect, it is a dissipation of capital gains. Second, there is a blunting of intellectual salients. No organization can make a deep thrust into new territory without a momentum of investigative effort behind it. Third, it breaks down the faith of young people in the research career as a way of life.

If research as a whole can be changed from a branchlike to a rootlike activity through the establishment of conducive conditions, the over-all quality of the scientific society can be immeasurably lifted. A new dimension of incentives would be added to the profession. To realize this transformation, there must be an infusion of purpose among the managements of all laboratories. Their operations must be driven by the spirit of solidarity expressed through a common concern for the growth of the researcher. This growth feature has been shown in Chapter 11 to be the basic drive among living creatures. Special laboratories isolated in competitive chinks and myopic crannies may ignore the common ideal for immediate short-term gains. They may close their eyes to the cumulative harm of their eventually self-defeating expedients. In the long run, however, continued profits to everyone can be made only in a society vested with a fair rate of growth. To maintain this tonus, every laboratory must make its contribution before it can retain the assurance of a continuing "cut" from research over the years.

Chapter 13

The Median Way

THE PRECEDING CHAPTERS have contrasted the simple black and white abstractions of science with the woolly gray totality of life. In the real world, everything is intermingled. Time merges, yesterday with today, the past with the future. Events do not have polished edges. Qualities shade into each other: strength into weakness, pleasure into pain, light into darkness, attraction into repulsion, strife into harmony. Man is a hodgepodge of diversities—his attachment to a hideous philosophy and to a lovely poem, his eagerness for the sublime and his nostalgia for the lascivious, his shared pains of physical desire and of nauseating satiety.

Gainful progress to society can be expected only from the integrated growth of the totality. An overpowering furtherance of a single segment without regard to the otherwise harmonious whole is but a cancerous disproportionment. Because of the intricate anastomoses of reality one cannot extricate oneself from the unit of which he is a part. Consequently, if we are to establish ourselves, we must establish others. In this statement lies the fount of social wisdom. Its realization in organized research constitutes the germ of leadership.

Organized research involves a sociological fusion of varying temperaments and motivations. The problem of the director centers on how he as a single element within the unit can guide it toward a predetermined objective. To do this, he must first gain a position of versatile leverage. In applying the lever he must recognize that he is primarily a coordinating influence shaping a social instrument of investigative coherence. This does not imply that he should relinquish his authority. Organized effort is cemented together through applied prerogatives. In times of stability, the leader should clothe his power in deliberate, refined, and velvety persuasion. In times of crises he must bare it in decisive, audacious, and at times even arbitrary actions. Power therefore must reside in his personage. As Winston Churchill sadly learned from his less-experienced days, one should not "attempt a major task from a subordinate position."

In this connection the millennia-old Indian Panchatantra stories spoke about Bull, the king's janitor, who after being cuffed about by Strong Tooth, the merchant, thought:

> Indulge no angry, shameless wish
> To hurt, unless you can:
> The chick pea, hopping up and down
> Will crack no frying pan.

However, the profitable use of power over individuals with initiative and self-reliant thinking requires skill, care, and consideration. The effective director of research does not dominate; he motivates. He does not impose force; he injects centralizing stimulants. His art is subtle, his method oblique. He follows the advice of Lao-tze: "Rule a country as you would fry a small fish."

In the manipulation of controls, distinction should be made between levels of knowledge and levels of synthesis. These should be related to the proper measure of authority. Let us dwell on the matter for an excursionary moment. The higher the echelon, the greater the inherent power of command. At what point should the jurisdiction for various decisions be administered? This is the heart of the controversy on centralization versus decentralization. An analysis of the question would suggest that centralization of authority does not necessarily mean the centralization of its administration. A confusion will lead to a burdensome bureaucracy and a cumbersome overhead. Authority and its administration should be considered separately. The administrative functions of rule-making, licensing, investigative and directing powers should be effected at the appropriate level of synthesis.

A level of synthesis means the place in the hierarchy at which all of the facts and factors are combined to produce a composite area picture. The area picture is then transferred to the next echelon which adds new considerations, resulting in an amalgam of a still larger order. In the congealing of a hierarchical decision, all echelons participate although only one finally makes it. Echelons not synthetic in this respect are noncontributory and should be abolished. Mere supervision or exercise of authority without contribution to further composition is not a sound reason for existence.

Neither should the limited span of control, so popular an index among management-conscious concerns, justify the interposition of intermediary channels in a research organization. With personnel capable of independent operation, the looser system of Sears Roebuck has considerable attractiveness. At Sears there have been as many as forty-two major executives reporting to one supervisor. In all, there were only six echelons. This is in contrast to du Pont with its thirteen rungs of command. Despite their divergence in social structure, both companies are doing very well.

The administration of authority over matters below one's own level of synthesis should be exercised with restraint. The statement is particularly appropriate since mastery of a discipline has no necessary bearing on the level of authority or of synthesis. Pre-eminence can be found anywhere, depending upon the particular skill under consideration. Questions should be referred as much as possible directly to the individual with the appropriate degree of competence.

The administration of authority should be exercised at the lowest levels of synthesis which are cognizant of the factors involved in the particular cases. Assignment of this activity to a higher echelon will lead to a top-heavy bureaucracy, and relegation to a lower echelon will result in an incomplete answer. There should accordingly be an appropriate administration of authority at all echelons, depending upon the nature of the question.

Executives should recognize their own limited range of knowledge. They should not imagine that their sensitivity to the subtle ramifications of a scientific innovation equips them with the insight into plotting an experimental path to that discovery. That a person enjoys eggs does not mean he can lay one.

The assumption should also be avoided that the researcher proceeds in the same manner as the director in attacking a problem and that the only difference is a more detailed technical competence on the part of the researcher. Based on such misconceptions, imprudent management frequently maps out a detailed experimental plan to be followed according to a prescribed schedule. This is hardly conducive to efficiency in research. Approaches to research problems are affairs of artistry to a large extent. Within broad limits no two scientists paint with the same strokes and one cannot dictate the mannerisms of the other.

Proficiency is not restricted to technical disciplines. There are also the important functional specialists who, in addition to their normal duties, perform great service for their associates. They include the father confessors, the peacemakers, the social leaders, the inspirers, as well as the less fortunate scapegoats and butts for jokes. Regardless of organizational position, these individuals frequently are the primary foci for action during periods of special needs. Attention upon them has evolved through informal associations, independent of formal authority and chain of command. These channels must be kept open.

Decentralization is easier said than done. There are loud magnanimous declarations among executives of their "letting the operators do the job." But in most instances when they do "decentralize," their minds are a mess of worry over the outcome. They install a host of cross-checks and security valves to insure that the threat of any deviation from established predictions would be immediately eliminated. Such executives have decentralized neither in fact nor in spirit.

To be intimately versed in the technique of decentralization, the executive must have a sense of the Taoist doctrine of inaction. Accomplishment is attained through the art of doing nothing. This is a somewhat difficult idea to put across, because so many people are quick to confuse it with loafing. But we may get a glimpse of the notion from Chuang-tze:

> The student of knowledge (aims at) learning day by day;
> The student of Tao (aims at) losing day by day.
>> By continual losing
>> One reaches doing nothing (laissez-faire)
>> By doing nothing everything is done.
> He who conquers the world often does so by doing nothing.
> When one is compelled to do something,
> The world is already beyond his conquering.

Chuang-tze continues to remind us, "Who can make muddy water clear? But if left alone, it will gradually become clear by itself. Who can secure a state of repose? But let time go on and the state of repose will gradually set in."

Let us leave the diversionary discussion on managerial levels and return to the Median Way. The desirability of a median position in contrast to an extreme has been put forth by many people. Aristotle's Doctrine of the Golden Mean proposes that moral virtues lie in the intermediate state between the extremes of excess and deficiency. The Platonic extension goes on to elaborate that good things in the world are mixed. In action one must know the right place to stop, not a jot more, not a tittle less.

The Golden Mean is not necessarily an arithmetic position between extremes. It is not a quantitative matter but a qualitative comparison against standard values. One acquires moral goodness by training until he hits the right balance between the extremes. The mean itself is not a static center but requires constant adjustment to shifting conditions. This idea of the mean has influenced the positivistic systems of ethics in modern times, especially behaviorism and pragmatism.

Confucius advanced a generally similar concept. Like Aristotle he suggests neither too much nor too little but just enough. The Master Confucius illustrated the point thus: "When the solid outweighs the ornamental, we have boorishness; when the ornamental outweighs the solid, we have superficial smartness. Only from a proper blending of the two will we have a higher type of man."

Even in the case of present-day industrial profits, we note the practical wisdom of successful corporations in the Median Way. H. Maurer says that the managers of Sears Roebuck stores are criticized for too much as well as too little profit. An excessive profit may mean the loss of potential customers, the poor paying of employees, or undue skimping on repair and maintenance. The territorial vice-presidents of the parent concern make it a point to prevent local managers from maximizing temporary profits.

Not only must the optimum be exhibited in quantity and space but also in time. According to Barnard, the art of executive decisions consists in "not deciding questions that are not now pertinent, in not deciding prematurely, in not making decisions that cannot be made effective,

and in not making decisions that others should make." Failure to anticipate the need for a future decision and to gauge the appropriate length
of time necessary for incubation and implementation accounts for many
an executive's "missing the boat." But, of course, worry itself should be
permitted neither lead time nor lag time. Timeliness is a cornerstone
of executive success and good health.

The Confucian version of the Golden Mean introduces the idea of
centrality (*Chung*) and harmony (*Ho*) as the inescapable law of our
existence. Man is united to the universal order by the property of central
harmony. If one's sorrow and joy, anger and pleasure, and other emotions
are present in proper proportions, central harmony is established within
the individual.

Chung and *Ho* are well illustrated in the organic architecture of
Matthew Nowicki and Frank Lloyd Wright. These modern architects
show a lively cognizance of the ramifications of function, form, and
human aspirations. Their designs are congenial integrations of all these
aspects of life. In developing the sketches for the library and museum
near the North Carolina State House in Raleigh, Nowicki respected the
local sentiment for provincial classicism. Similarly when he collaborated
in the design of the capital of East Punjab he absorbed the complex
richness of the Hindu personality and life. Into the functionality of
buildings he infused the concordant subjective as well as the objective
ingredients that make them organic. Wright's introduction of the
garden into the interior of his prairie homes followed the same respect
for harmony. It reflects an adjustment to the human desire to embrace
nature.

Mumford contrasted the buildings of Nowicki and Wright with those
of the United Nations. The dominance of the Secretariat Building over
the General Assembly Building evidences little regard for the hopes of
billions of people that the United Nations would not be doomed to a
limbo of paper work. Furthermore there is no functional requirement
for the impressive height of the Secretariat Building. The glass façade
is uneconomical in maintenance. The large unbroken slab at the end
walls reduces the efficiency of the work inside. In a desire to provide
aesthetic purity the architects sacrificed function and symbol. These
were Mumford's analyses. If he is correct, we would say that the buildings of the United Nations lack *Chung* and *Ho*.

Harmony does not imply uniformity. It is more like a ballet—an artistic and pleasing blending of a multitude and diversity of notes and motions. To press uniformity is like singing a song on one pitch or executing a dance on one stance. Harmony is not only compatible with differences but without them there can be no harmony. A harmonious group, therefore, is a composition of people with different talents, tastes, and tempers, all occupying their places of expertness and enriching the whole through their proper contributions. It is not a stereotypic monotone of followers resulting from the suppression of deviations and the subjugation of personalities.

According to an extension of *Chung* and *Ho,* if a man wants anything he must admit something of the opposite. Lao-tze expressed it thus: "The recognition of beauty implies the idea of ugliness and the recognition of good implies the idea of evil." To stimulate development the director must admit some basic research. To encourage basic research he must include some development. To foster discipline he must allow freedom. To guarantee freedom he must preserve order. To mature reason he must entertain mysticism. To fertilize imagination he must be illumined by reason. While tending to the rigors of austerity and thrift, he must bend his ears to Venus and Bacchus. Nobility must be beveled with humor, strength with relaxation, chivalry with propriety.

He must at all times beware the attainment of the extreme. Excesses bring sad consequences, as stretching a bow beyond its full and tempering the knife edge beyond its sharpest. Fire is its quenching. Probably influenced by his deep knowledge of and intimate feeling for Asian art and philosophy, Malraux had this to say about that extreme of extremes (the Absolute), "The Absolute is the last resort of the tragic man, the only solace, because it alone can consume—even if the whole man is consumed with it—the deepest feeling of dependence, remorse at being oneself." In the opposite direction, Merton considers despair to be the "absolute extreme of self-love." A man in despair refuses to accept any help from anyone else for the sheer "rotten luxury of knowing himself to be lost." A man must be cautious in success but hopeful in crisis. To be arrogant implies the limit is reached; to be humble suggests that it is not and, hence, to increase in strength. And we may add, with Thucydides, that "of all the manifestations of power, restraint impresses men most."

There is the familiar advice about having one's cake and eating it too. One cannot simultaneously retain all the extreme advantages in life. He cannot be a researcher at the bench, synthesizing pharmaceuticals for the alleviation of human suffering or conjuring mathematical phantasms for bridging the wave and the corpuscular natures of light, and at the same time be a director of research. He cannot be the authority in a specialized discipline of learning yet have the general cognizance of the many broad fields in which an executive must participate. He cannot unleash the aggressiveness in a subordinate for the good of his organization at certain intervals and expect to suppress it completely in the interim. He cannot insist on orthodoxy without a diminution in creativity. The director of research must not mourn the loss of incompatible ideals and irreconcilable extremes. The shadows must be accepted with the light. He can only hope that his compromises will move the parent organization closer to its over-all objective.

One of the contemporary excesses to which science is a material contributor is the Machine Age. To bring this extreme back to the median is a crying task before humane leaders. The reason that the present century is fittingly called the Machine Age is not the abundance of machines, nor is it man's dependency on them. It lies in man's changed attitude. Instead of looking upon machines merely as aids toward the attainment of his ideals, man is now being spiritually overwhelmed. He is beginning to emulate the characteristics of the machine itself. What makes a machine "good" is being adopted as the criteria of man's good. Like the machine's sole concern with means, man too is becoming engrossed in means in lieu of ends. Consequences are taking the place of purposes.

Imitating the machine's cold objectivity, many executives regard objectivity in dealing with their fellow men a cardinal virtue. Imitating the machine's impersonal responses, many bosses consider human-heartedness an executive weakness. Imitating the emotionless crushing of a careless hand that crosses the machine's way, the tycoon pulverizes human obstacles that trespass on his empire. The criteria of economy, severity, precision, repetitive reliability, and simple essentiality without complicating subjectivity have been successfully applied to machines. The same criteria are now being pelted about as indices of an employee's desirability. The Machine Age is narrowing the human response, restricting the human choice, and depersonalizing the human virtues. Like a hermit crab shaping its body to the conformity of the dead shell it has picked up, social patterns today are being molded along the confines of soulless machines.

The problem of the machine's invasion of the human soul, to follow the thoughts of the Austrian poet Rilke, revolves around the cost of redemption by a share of man's spirit for the demands of the inanimate. Max Plowman asked the key question: "How much of the mechanized utility placed at our disposal by scientific discovery are we able to incorporate in our lives without damage to our distinctive human nature?" In anticipation of his dilemma, Lao-tze had given conservative advice in the story of a peasant who refused to hear more about an irrigation device which Tse-kung told him would "water a hundred fields in one day." "My master has taught me," the peasant replied, "that a person who has cunning gadgets is cunning in his affairs. Being cunning in his affairs, he is also cunning in his heart. Being cunning in his heart, he loses something and his spirit becomes restless. With his spirit restless, Tao flies away."

Thinking of man as a machine cannot help quickening the atrophy of his human capacities. There must be a return to human-heartedness, wholeness, and balance. Only then can there be true objectivity, which people demand but often confuse. Does not objectivity include every aspect that bears on the question at hand? Is not the human being himself one of the factors? Values another? Tolstoi in *War and Peace* posed the problem of objectivity in the case of the captive Pierre Bezukhov before one of Napoleon's generals, Marshal Davoust.

> At first glance when Davoust had only raised his head from the papers where human affairs and lives were indicated by numbers, Pierre was merely a circumstance, and Davoust could have shot him without burdening his conscience with an evil deed, but now he saw in him a human being. . . .

Another extreme which needs discretionary handling in a management-conscious country is the overemphasis on systemization of human activities. Mumford traced the general occurrence of this "fallacy of systems." He pointed out how the world has been subjected to the persistent though well-meaning efforts of "system-makers" and "system-mongers" since the seventeenth century who attempt to organize the entire life of a community on the basis of some limiting principle of the moment, as if "wholesale limitations would do justice to the condition of man." After painful adjustments, each of these systems was to experience the loss of its purity, forced by the necessity of compromise and modification to meet the demands of the world.

Introduction of systems, it seems, is nearly always in the form of extremes, disregarding the Golden Mean of Aristotle and Confucius. Now and then arise men of nobility who recognize the beauty and prerequisites of balance and harmony in human affairs. St. Ignatius Loyola is a good example. When the system-conscious Church of the Middle Ages encouraged the one-sided development of the self to such an extent that it no longer was able to assimilate life in its unity, Loyola founded spiritual exercises in harmony with the nature of man. He recognized that violent commitment even to virtue itself is an extreme that perverts the soul. His efforts were directed toward bringing that segment of virtue within the greater whole of life.

In order to avoid the extreme and gain a position of universal leverage, the executive must first recognize the relationships of the different factors in the total setting. He must adjust the pulse beats of the laboratory to those of the parent institution. He must understand the multifarious jostling of opposing and competing forces, the nature and the vectors of these extremes. He must then select a focus which can reach out in all directions, to quote Mencius, "standing in the center under Heaven in order to hold the people in place within the four seas." He must be familiar with the motivating agents within his sphere of influence. He must also be aware of those beyond his immediate reach.

Extremes within his manipulative range are rendered complementary to his directional purpose by juxtaposing opposing forces. In this way they are harmonized and made useful. When they lie beyond his sway, however, he has no recourse but to await serenely their mutual resolution into a desirable resultant or a harmless neutralization. If he is patient, this should not take long. It is in the nature of inordinate people to live by combat. They search out their own destruction. They remind us of Carl Sandburg's heroes:

> In a Colorado graveyard
> Two men lie now in one grave.
> They shot it out in a jam over who owned
> One corner lot—over a piece of real estate.

They shot it out: It was a perfect duel.
They cleansed the world of each other,
Each horizontal in an identical grave
Had his bones cleaned by the same maggots.
They sleep now as accommodating neighbors.

If one extends himself beyond his natural spans to crush an extreme, he no longer occupies a median position. He himself joins the peripheral jungle. It is unfortunate that there are many people who feel that their pre-eminence in the world requires constant public controversies.

A clear distinction should be made between the method of balancing power and of centralizing influence. In the former case, the goal of the individual is to become eventually the strongest in the assemblage. He himself is always contending for the extreme of extreme positions. In the meantime, in order to prevent his own destruction by another power similarly motivated, he enlaces himself with alliances and incites new enemies against the competitor, who is thereby made inferior. In the practice of centralizing influence, however, the person is not seeking pre-eminence. He is interested in the harmony of the total society. He shifts balance by the proper positioning of the fulcrum. In the peaceful progression of a well-poised society, he does not disturb the balance by jumping forth to an encampment of dominance. Inasmuch as unmitigatedly ambitious people do exist, he must control and blend them into a harmonious unity. Otherwise the system will fall apart from their eternal mortal jousting. He does not create a balance of power for his own selfish advancement. He encourages an equilibrium for the good of the whole.

The executive cannot afford the personal gratification of hogging the limelight, for this, too, would be a manifestation of extreme which converts him into a contender of limited survival. He must share the honors that chance his way. As Lao-tze has put it, "He who raises himself on tiptoe cannot stand firm." When vanity presses relentlessly, he should further meditate on the comments of Lord Oliver of France, who observed during the Middle Ages that some men are like apes. They never cease jumping from bough to bough until they reach the highest point in the tree, thereby baring their behind for full view by those below. Or he may cogitate on a page from the Taoist books about the dangers of a fine reputation:

Cinnamon is edible, so the cinnamon tree is cut down. Ch'i oil is useful, so the Ch'i tree is gashed. On the other hand, a sacred oak, whose wood was good for nothing and accordingly was spared, said to the axman in a dream, "For a long time I have been learning to be useless. On several occasions I was nearly destroyed, but I have now succeeded in being useless, which is of greatest use to me. If I were useful, could I have become so great?

Chuang-tze reminds us that the world knows only the usefulness of the useful, but does not know the usefulness of the useless.

The Median Way is also a path of reasonableness. A proposition must not only be correct; it must also be reasonable. The logician who feels self-righteous posts a stand of inanimate inflexibility; the reasonable person suspects he may be in error, being therefore always in the right. He recognizes the frailty of knowledge and the transience of strength. We can observe from our everyday experience how it is that the ingratiating and reasonable man is usually the one who is hopeful that at least a part of his proposition will be adopted. It is the one who envisions little chance who is usually self-righteous and uncompromising. Profundity in reasonableness is preferable to profundity in reasoning.

The skilful executive therefore is never an extremist. He does not plume himself with the importance of his office. He is always a reasonable fellow. Of all the gifts proffered him, he retains only the pivotal one of centralizing capability. He recognizes the dangers of the sudden application of large forces to the human society. Action based on massive doses pays the price of flexibility and adaptability. Biochemists have shown nature's preference for stout gradualness. Instead of being released in a destructively explosive fashion, the energy from ingested foods is liberated in useful, life-providing tiny packets through a succession of metabolic reactions and cycles, coupled to each other directly, indirectly, and through bypaths, involving hundreds of related compensating mechanisms. So it is with social life.

The research leader should eschew the old Newtonian rule of management: to every action there is an equal and opposite reaction. Instead, he should motivate his network of interactions so that to every action there is an equal and organic assimilation.

Part V

The

Assimilation

of

Modern

Science

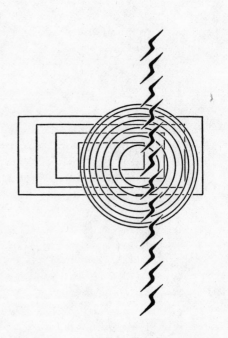

Chapter 14

The Synthetic Leap

BEGINNING WITH THE FIFTEENTH CENTURY there was a general transition in European thought. Part of the metamorphosis involved venomous religious controversies. By about the sixteenth and seventeenth centuries overzealous theologians had placed delicately balanced chips on their spiritual shoulders. In order to give increasing credence to their surety they would refuse to admit error, even on statements not necessarily bearing on morality or fundamental dogma. Nobody could teach them anything. They did not consider things beyond their sphere of interest of Being, Essence, Cause, and Ends worthwhile. Nothing had any significance except as it was obtained by the black-and-white system laid down by them.

It was in these circumstances that science first clashed with theology. The famous controversy concerning the rotation of the earth around a second-rate sun exemplifies the nature of the prevailing opinions. Let us compare the view of Galileo (1564–1642) with that of St. Thomas Aquinas (ca. 1225–1274). To St. Thomas motion is a branch of metaphysics and is explained as "the act of that which is in potentiality, as such." The reason for the existence of motion is that things seek their "proper" place or direction. Everything has its "proper" place. The "proper" location due to fire "in respect to its form (is) to be in a

The Tao of Science

higher place." Whether or not such statements are "true" depends upon their consistency with a particular world view which is supported by data supplied through divine revelation. The Scholastic doctrine can be metaphysically "true" in this respect and yet empirically "false." As far as the motion of heavenly bodies is concerned, the given dogma states them to be perfect and unalterably in a circle. The reasoning extended as follows: Elemental air, fire, water, and earth move in straight lines to their respective "proper" places. Air and fire move upwards. In contrast, water and earth move downwards. Straight line movements are thus characterized with "contraries." The heavenly bodies, however, move in a circular fashion. Accordingly, their movements must be without contraries. But Aristotle has shown metaphysically that all generated objects arise from their contraries. They also fall back into them. Since the heavenly bodies have no contraries, they must therefore be incorruptible.

Galileo attacked this theory of incorruptibility in his *System of the World*. He relied on observations in place of metaphysical disputations. Through his telescope he saw heavenly generation and corruption in the appearance and dissolution of dense and obscure materials in the skies. Galileo felt that sense evidence cannot be wished away by theoretical deductions. His associates at the University of Padua argued philosophically at length against his conclusions but refused to look through his telescope. Despite many suppressions and setbacks the intellectual absolutism of scholastic metaphysics over all phases of human thought was gradually overthrown. Theology found its proper sphere of activity and science was permitted to mature.

But modern science is beginning to forget the labor of her birth and Galileo's revolt against the scholastic trammels to establish "things as are and seen" in preference to "things as abstracted and conceived." Resplendent in her attainments and power, she is ascending the very same throne of the intellectual monarch she deposed.

Science now appears to be dictating the intellectual fashions of the day. If a plan is not prepared according to the scientific method, it is considered unreliable. If a question cannot be tested by science, it is considered meaningless. If traditional institutions are slow to adopt the scientific way, they are considered backward. If a mode of life is not comprehendible by science, it is considered old-fashioned. As a result of these intrusions, the certitude of purpose in the scheme of things begins to waver. Means are being homogenized with ends.

Many scientists are on the threshold of emulating theologians of the sixteenth century. Some are beginning to develop a pugnacity that bespeaks a deep uncertainty of brittle pride. Others are transgressing beyond their limited compass of competence. Still others seem not to care a doit that the unitary purpose of culture is being blunted and that the wholeness of meaning and the very tradition of a cooperative society are being disintegrated. If encouraged along the current trends, science may soon reach the point of diminishing usefulness to humanity. To retain her contributing relevancy is an important problem of the twentieth century.

The doctrine "Science for science's sake" is symptomatic of the scholarly blinkers which are diminishing her potentialities of greater service to man. By adhering to this maxim, science is cutting herself off from her source of significance. Chesterton wrote quite pungently on this score. He found it "extremely difficult to believe that a man who is obviously uprooting mountains and dividing seas, tearing down temples and stretching out hands to the stars, is really a quiet old gentleman who only asks to indulge his harmless old hobby and follow his harmless old nose." When an atom is split and a hundred thousand lives are smothered and the world is thrown into terrible anxiety for centuries thereafter, how can the layman believe that the splitting of the atom is a great and commendable accomplishment and the resulting destructiveness a blameless inadvertence. "It is hard to enter into the feelings of a man who regards a new heaven and a new earth in the light of a by-product. But undoubtedly it is to this almost eerie innocence of the intellect that the great men of the great scientific period owed their enormous power and triumph," concluded Chesterton.

The primacy of the spiritual and social well-being of man has always been the measure of nobility. Man's conviction in the loftiness of this purpose has been repeatedly demonstrated through charitable sacrifices and bloody martyrdoms. It takes a devilish depraving of man's goodness to rationalize this ingrained voice of conscience into an incidental happenstance. In these times of insecurity in the wisdom of our intelligentsia, there needs to be a reappraisal of the doctrine of "Science for science's sake" and its twin, "Knowledge for knowledge's sake." Should science be regarded as merely amusement for the erudite few? Should it be a floating iceberg of drifting data? Or should it be a means of infusing man's perceptions into his feelings for his fellows and his consciousness of life?

We may recall the frivolous yet tired society of Louis XV grasping for pleasure and rest, which led to the *"l'art pour l'art"* of the rococo. The contemplative peace of the ivory tower was bought at the price of understanding the human order. It was not that, after surveying one's capabilities of service to mankind, the ivory tower was selected as the most fertile locale for one's peculiar contributions. Nor was it the belief that the welfare of the world indeed was contingent on the excellence of art. If this had been so, it would not have been "art for art's sake," but "art for man's sake through art." Thus, *l'art pour l'art* represented a revolt against all external bonds, a refusal to participate in human strivings, a romantic evasion of duty. Perhaps the present materialistic version of a frivolous yet tired society cannot but engender an atmosphere of science for science's sake. But we can take hope in the precedent that following the rococo, art soon revitalized her intimacy to life with the active expressions of Beethoven, Stendhal, and Delacroix. Perhaps the same will happen for twentieth century science.

The current emphasis upon science is but another instance of the recurring spotlight that history plays on various scenes of its panorama. These are too significant to be called fads, although if judged against the background of eons of time, the term may well apply. Instead they are called movements. What the newfangled enthusiasts have actually achieved was merely to focus attention on a particular thing, which had been torn out of context, bloody and rootless for the world to stare at and wonder. Tinseled glamor is invariably injected in the claim that a new elixir has been discovered which will dissolve man's myriad torments. We are invited to concentrate on the panacea. Phrenology, astrology, the mechanical, chemical, Darwinian, Rousseauian, Freudian . . . all have had their heyday.

In actual point of fact, there is little novelty in these nostrums. The enduring thinkers have discussed them exhaustively and wisely. However, the picture drawn by the wise men shone with the contextural truth and beauty of reality. In it had been entertained not only the particular question emphasized in the fashion of the day but all adjacent and distal ramifications intermeshing in the totality of life.

As far as the place of research in the scheme of things is concerned, Confucius advanced a preferable precept for us to follow:

> The ancients, who wished to preserve the clear and good character of the world, first set about to regulate their national life. In order to regulate their national life, they cultivated their family life. In order to cultivate their family life, they rectified their personal life. In order to rectify their personal life, they elevated their heart. In order to elevate their heart they made their will sincere. In order to make their will sincere, they enlightened their mind. In order to enlighten their mind, they conducted research. Their research being conducted, their mind was enlightened. Their mind being enlightened, their will was made sincere. Their will being sincere, their heart was elevated. Their heart being elevated, their personal life was rectified. Their personal life being rectified, their family life was cultivated. Their family life being cultivated, their national life was regulated. Their national life being regulated, the good and clear character of the world was preserved and peace and tranquillity reigned thereafter.

True and lasting progress in civilization is made by integrated and balanced sequences. The longer and more intensive the cultural skewness, the more difficult will it be for succeeding generations to bring the momentum of history back into kilter. The stanza from Pope's *Essay on Man* is eloquent in this respect:

> Vice is a monster of such frightful mien
> As to be hated, needs but to be seen;
> Yet seen too oft, familiar with her face
> We first endure, then pity, then embrace.

The long brooding on the disjunction of science from life caused Tolstoi to remark that "Science is meaningless because it gives no answer to our question, the only one important for us: 'What shall we do and how shall we live?'"

Weber analyzed the manner in which Tolstoi came to this conclusion. For many years Tolstoi's thoughts revolved around the meaningfulness of death. They finally led him to the answer that for civilized man, death has no purpose. This is due to the fact that civilized man appears as only one step in a long "progress." No matter how "advanced" civilization is, there is always someone ahead of him. Consequently, nobody stands at the peak of this advancement. Civilized man therefore never has had enough of life. He may be "tired of life" but never "satiated with life." Whatever experience he undergoes is only provisional and never definitive. Death then becomes an empty phenomenon. And because death is senseless, civilized life itself, shaped by the "progressiveness" of science, becomes senseless. The religious peasants and the people of Abraham's time do not suffer this despair. For these simple folks, the interpretation of life has been given. There are no enigmas. Having lived a full life with what was offered, they have had enough of the organic cycle. As a result, they die "old and satiated with life."

It would be asking too much of science to provide an answer for life. Science herself does not pursue such questions. Let us take the natural sciences. These fields of learning operate on the premise that it is worthwhile knowing the ultimate laws of cosmic phenomena. The search for these laws is, in turn, based on the suppositions of cause and effect, the validity of logic, and the other expedients of science. As shown in the earlier chapters, these postulates can hardly be considered clear and firm. It is inconceivable that science would extend her assumptions to even further orders of remoteness involving the worth of the universe itself and the meaning of life.

Let us take medicine. Doctors assume that life is worth saving. Despite the certain fatality of an illness in question, the agony of the attendant suffering, and the desperate imploring of the patient for the relieving quietude of death, a doctor will not touch the scalpel to the thread of life. Whether life is worth living and for how long are not the concerns of medicine.

Continuing along this vein, Weber showed that aesthetics does not inquire why there should be works of art. It does not question whether or not art is a handmaiden of the devil and therefore hostile to God but just determines the conditions under which art does flourish.

In similar manner, jurisprudence does not ask whether there should be laws. It just analyzes whether certain rules are binding under current juristic thought.

Historical and cultural studies do not evaluate whether or not civilization is worthwhile. They merely teach us how to dissect and understand historical and cultural events in terms of their origins.

Thus it is that Tolstoi's original question "How shall we arrange our lives?" is avoided by our technical knowledge. But this does not mean that science is without influence on decisions that relate to life itself. It may mean that the positive approach of science is insensible to the subtleties of the Undifferentiated Aesthetic Continuum. This has been granted in Chapter 9. It does not exclude the possibility that man can participate in the superrational realm by other means. This too has been covered in the same chapter which advanced the means of no-knowledge. The thesis was argued that the rational knowledge of science, with its positive approach, should join with intuitive knowledge and no-knowledge, with their negative approach, in the totality of man's conscience and feelings. What modern science is unwittingly doing is alienating intuitive knowledge and no-knowledge, with their attendant negative ways to enlightenment, from man's sensibilities by the imposition of rational knowledge, with its positive tactics, as the final test of reality. Paradoxically, it is precisely in the use of the negative method in this instance—an approach not recognized by science—that the fragmentation of man is engendered by science. In this manner modern science composes an answer to Tolstoi's question and contributes to his uneasiness concerning the apparent futility of life.

This analysis of the tenor of modern science is not meant to echo the prophets of doom. We find such characters in all ages, bemoaning the sickness of their centuries. Thirty-six hundred years ago, the Sumerians wrote about the gloom and misery of man. In style with the Roman Tacitus, pessimism has seeped into the writings and speeches of many of our greatest authors and thinkers. Before him the poet Horace had sharply asked: "Our fathers, more vile than our grandfathers, begot us who are even viler and we shall bring forth a progeny more degenerate still?" The current literature—Spengler, Huxley, Santayana, Toynbee, Eliot, Porter—is full of such depressing thoughts. Even science has its share of despairing prophecies. There is the terrible Darwinian base of human activity, the survival of the fittest, committing man to the fight of the jungle. There is the hopeless second law of thermodynamics which says that the universe is continually running down, condemned inexorably by the increasing entropy.

On the contrary, we should not find anything hopeless in the temporary swing of a pendulum away from the center. The farther away it is, the sooner it ought to reverse itself. "Reversal is the nature of the Tao." So it is with the alienation of prodigal science from society. She is bound to come home. The earlier her disillusionment, of course, the sooner will she return. The sooner her return, the better for man. So let us get on with our task of persuasion. We should not share the sentiments of Eliot that the world will end "not with a bang but a whimper." We much prefer for this purpose Havelock Ellis' "Sunset is the promise of dawn."

The reflowing of science into the stream of human consciousness entails a moderation on the part of science in the very comportment that was responsible for her present prominence. Let us trace the place of science on the human scene. During early historical times, science was not segregated from the general bag of human techniques. She was just one of the many practical aids to life. Astronomy was undertaken to devise a calendar to help navigators and farmers. Later astronomy changed into astrology, the divination of human fate. It nevertheless remained an offspring of people's requirements. So also originated the other disciplines. Biology sprang from medicine, chemistry from the industrial arts, certain mathematics from magic formulations, and others from trade and commerce. During those days the axioms, customs, and activities of science were intermingled with those of the world and man.

Originally science attempted to look at entire phenomena and understand them in toto. But the progress was slow. As delineated in Chapter 8, the analytical technique of abstraction was developed. Segments were abstracted from the whole and examined. When the abstractions were comprehended, frequently only in their general shapes, there was always a temptation to interpret the whole reality in terms of the abstractions. The imposing symbolic structure of Medieval Europe in which every event was seen as a witness to a host of ultimate meanings is now being replaced by an equally imposing symbolic structure: Instead of revelations and essences, there are now the positronium, psyche, and so on. Everything in the world is to be described in terms of the new ultimate particles and forces.

As a result of her abstraction complex, science began to dissociate her thoughts from the parent reality of mankind from which she sprang. She wanted to be left alone to play with her artificial worlds, creating things and systems that often do not harmonize with the scheme of life and upsetting the equilibrium of the world in most explosive ways. For these reasons R. Guenon refers to modern science as the "degenerate vestiges" of the ancient traditional knowledge. Wiser scientists are beginning to realize that a specialist is but an abstraction of man, a personality out of context. They are beginning to appreciate Toynbee's conclusions that "there is no correlation between progress in technique and progress in civilization." Their souls clamor in their native humility for a return to the complete man. Yet to be men as men, they must cease being a particular kind of men. They cannot be men as scientists. They must shake off their servitude to the chains of abstracted and rational thought. They must control the scientific implements, put them in their proper perspective and lose them in the intimacy of their total experience as men.

Life flowed on quite well before science matured into her modern form. Great nations had been established; beautiful structures had been built; wonderful cultures had been developed; men had been happy; souls had gone to heaven—all without the aid of modern science. But modern science is an ingredient which can add new zest to life. The task before us is to emulsify this component into the older and profounder art of life.

We can hardly afford an aggravation of the widening intellectual gulf between science and other facets of human activity. We should confess a growing concern over the recurrence of hostile issues that are splitting the scientists themselves into various camps. The recent marked increase in the odd group of functional specialists who use political methods for advancing their scientific positions—the political physicists, the political chemists, the political professors, the political doctors, and other politically lacquered scientists—has poured fuel on this fire of dissension. We should remember that the loss of the will of functional groups to cooperate has been one of the main causes of the disintegration of great civilizations in the past. We should regain the spontaneity of intuitive cooperation.

In directing his activities along the path of human-heartedness, man cannot succeed by restricting his compass to rational and intuitive knowledge. He must enrich his reservoir of no-knowledge. The requirement does not stem from the inability of rational and intuitive knowledge, if practiced to perfection, to attain the objective of human-heartedness. It is necessitated by the fact that man always falls short of his ideal and fails to exploit his utmost capabilities. For a very practical reason, therefore, man has been taught to aim high, failing which he still reaches a laudable level of accomplishment. So it is with the pursuit of no-knowledge. If attained, no-knowledge provides him not only with a sensitive and responsive communion with his fellow men but also with his fellow creatures. But characteristically human again, man will not reach such a high state of excellence. Falling short, however, he may still acquire the sense of human-heartedness toward men.

Relinquishing the intellectual throne for the life of a commoner is a hard chore for science after three hundred years of free ranging and a hundred years of lordship. We can fully appreciate her reluctance to make the sacrifice. Yet she should remember that when Christ asked the rich man to give what he had to the poor, he was not thinking particularly about the poor. It was the rich man who, choked in his plenitude of physical wealth, was in need of help. To soothe and guide science in her difficult yet inevitable decision will be the principal aesthetic contribution of the scientific leaders of today.

Chapter 15

The Philosopher-Executive

LET US DISTILL the previous deliberations. We have touched upon the ancient roots of modern science. We have uncovered the shaky uncertainties on which her facts and methodologies are grounded. We have observed the pitfalls in the use of logic, especially when shrouded in the ambiguities of language. We have alluded to the inability of science to clarify the deeper significance of life. We have hinted at a deepening wedge that the abstractive domination of modern science is driving between herself and humanity. At the same time, we have searched encouraging avenues for a renaissance of science in devotion to the welfare of man. There is the negative method of education, imparting a deep awareness of nature without jeopardizing the development of specialists. There is the Median Way of leadership. There are the reassessed contributions of organized research. There is the expanded freedom of growth in social effort. There is no-knowledge.

Our preface said something about the philosophical and aesthetic bases of research management. We have covered this in a diffused manner throughout the text. There are other touches to be added. Just what characteristics should executives in research ideally possess in order to gain the objectives delineated in the previous chapters? We shall now attempt to describe this personality.

The Tao of Science

An impression exists among some circles that a staff of renowned scientists has no particular need for exceptional leadership. The reputation of such an organization will sustain its chief. All that the presidency requires is a successful money procurer with a charming personality. In consonance with this attitude, too frequently a mediocre scholar has been shunted into the directorship of research institutions, because the "good men" have been retained at the individual investigative level. This way of thinking degenerates leaders into minor administrators of routine intellectual consequence. They provide no inspiration of great pith nor command any respect of significant moment.

Actually, the more expert the men in the organized effort, the more valuable are their skills, the more significant are their potential contributions, and the more exacting is their need for wise management. A deep concern must be given to the most effective employment of these precious talents. The more spirited the stallions, the more skilfully must the reins be handled. It is even said in the ancient Chinese *Book of History:* "In ruling over the people, I feel as if I were holding six horses with worn-out reins."

The direction of human beings is a matter of artistry, rather than procedures and formulae. For a simple analogy, we can draw on the study of Pareto on the effect of demand upon supply. With a community of a hundred persons, exchanging seven hundred products, he showed that 70,699 simultaneous equations were necessary to determine the prices which would balance out the demand and supply. With a population running into millions, the requisite equations would reach a completely unmanageable number. This led him to conclude that the market, not the mathematician, was the best guide to the management of prices.

In exercising research leadership the director is faced with far greater hurdles. He is dealing with subtle yet passionate commodities, human will, imagination, and mental constructions in a world of emotional capacities to implement distant events felt acutely. To make conditions conducive to a canalized direction requires an intimacy with the poetic and artistic features of life, as well as a skill in manipulating human labor and pecuniary power. There must be a penetration beneath the stilted managerial outlines of programs, budget, personnel, reporting, and systems of communication. Such topics form the pedagogic chants for the training of junior executives. By themselves, however, the administrative factors are like figures in Madame Tussaud's wax museum. They give a general idea of what the living form should resemble but nary a twitch of life. Pope's famous couplet is a useful summation:

> For forms of government let fools contest;
> Whate'er is best administer'd is best.

A lively direction of research dovetails diverse characters into a collective course of action. Let us see who some of these actors are.

There is the receptive type. He is highly dependent on others for help, constant support, and inspiration. He feels lost when left alone and is extremely sensitive to rebuffs. He is helpless at making definitive decisions. He scans the walls unendingly and cowers under the shelter of advisers and committees. He is paralyzed by doubt.

There is the exploiting type. Like the receptive individual, he, too, feels that the source of good is outside himself. However, the exploiter grabs, steals, and presses partisan advantage to the bitter end. Loyalty, humility, and respect are foreign to his make-up. He plagiarizes, indulges in senseless bickering over authorships, and bedecks himself with the honors that rightly belong to his associates. He compliments those he continues to exploit and disparages those squeezed dry.

There is the tight-lipped hoarding type. He squats behind the protective "no." Things outside his fortress are suspect; they have not been invented therein.

There is the marketing type. He is constantly concerned with what the traffic can bear. Exchange value rather than use value is his focus of attention. The program must be fashioned for highest remuneration from the current fashion train. How can he get on? How can the research be sold? What constitutes the most attractive wrapping? are his chief worries. The substance of the effort is purely ancillary.

There is the envenomed type who is continually jaded by his own ineptitude and sterility. He seeks to raise his relative position and reputation by constantly sneering at and looking for the worst weaknesses in his co-workers.

There is the frustrated type. He had once tasted the uplifting satisfaction of creativity but now is beginning to realize a drying up of his powers, being forever denied the ambrosial rewards reserved for the greats. Although he is still very capable and can contribute very significantly using the talents he does have, his mind is preoccupied with the recognition that he is just not quite good enough to be the great man he wants to be. He soon loses faith in himself and frequently winds up a leading fanatic in one cause or another.

There is the sincere creator. He is imbued with the ardor for new messages of increasing goodness for his fellow men, without particular concern for credit and honors. His potentialities and powers are fully developed to the limit of his natural ability to the advantage of society.

The list of behavioral types just presented partly follows Freud's and Fromm's discussions. We may incorporate other classifications, such as the delightful Taoist breakdown of smugs, snugs, and humpback (to borrow Lin Yu-tang's translation):

> Smugs are those people who having heard what their teacher says, feel very satisfied and very pleased with themselves. They think that they have learned the truth and do not realize that there was a time when no material universe existed.
>
> The snugs are lice on the bodies of hogs. They choose their abode in the long mane and hair of the hogs and believe themselves to be living in a grand palace with a big garden. They hide themselves in the corners, arm-pits, breasts and legs of the pigs and think that they are living in security. They do not realize that one day the butcher may come and rolling up his sleeves to lay hay under it and set fire to singe the pig and both themselves and the pig will be scorched to death. This is to live within the limitations of their own choice.
>
> The humpback was Emperor Shun. The mutton does not crave for the ants but the ants crave for mutton because of its rank smell. Emperor Shun had a rank character which attracted the people; the people loved him. Therefore, after he changed his capital three times and had moved to the plains of Teng, there were over a hundred thousand people who followed him. Emperor Yao heard of Shun's ability and put him in charge of a barren district, saying, "I hope that people who follow him there will receive the benefit of his rule." When Shun was put in charge of the barren district, he was already old, his eyesight and hearing were failing, but he was not allowed to retire.

Whether or not our coverage of personalities is complete is immaterial for our purpose. It suffices to point out that a laboratory is made up of quite diverse characters. To emulsify them into a smooth blend is not a job for the high-handed boss who sweeps everything before him. It is not a task for the old-line efficiency expert of charts and figures whose iridescence of life has long since been extinguished in the inkwell. It is not a chore for the flaccid Pollyanna who believes that forfeit of leadership through intellectual anarchy is the fountainhead of fruitful scientific management. It is not a charge for the inflexible scientist whose insistence on free creativity is distorted into a withdrawal from cooperation with other men. It is a task for the philosopher-executive.

The philosopher-executive extends his horizons beyond hard dollars, cold science, and inert plans. He must focus his determined purpose against the constantly shifting screen of politics, business, intellectual prejudices, scientific fashions, personality conflicts. In particular he is capable of handling the ever-recurring decisions involving conflicts in codes and desires. The laws of the land, the ethical tradition of his superiors, associates, and subordinates, the code of management, the aims of the parent organization, the humanitarian equity of the moment, the professional practices of the many disciplines represented are forever contending for dominant influence.

There is accordingly a continuing conflict of values confronting the executive in his judgments. A multiplicity of objectives vies for a scarcity of means. When the choice involves the mutual exclusion of conflicting codes, the greatest test of his sagacity arises. He has no guiding principle for the resolution of specific cases involving the juggling of differential abilities, priorities of demands, and probabilities of returns. As a consequence of these multifarious pressures toward varying ends, each involving multiple alternate means, full satisfaction rarely is meted out to any one side.

In cases of conflict, does the executive bludgeon through one plan? Such are the tactics of the tough tycoon. Or does he recall the old Chinese adage: When choosing between alternatives of grave import but involving high uncertainties, one should choose that path which if proven wrong results in the least harm? This is the safest solution. Or does he create a new action which dissolves the original conflict? This is the rare executive talent which requires an excursion into the regions of the not-not of the Buddhist truths in the higher sense discussed in Chapter 4. The same problems confront the manager of the most abstruse of research programs as well as the most practical of corporations.

Competition for limited rewards happens in the very best of families. The Cistercian monk Thomas Merton described episodes of contention among Jesus Christ's personally picked team: "More than once Jesus had to rebuke His Apostles who were wrangling among themselves and fighting for the first places in His Kingdom. Two of them, James and John, intrigued for the seats on His right and left hand in the Kingdom."

To discharge his various obligations in style, the philosopher-executive covers the integrated whole of experience with a triple insight—the dreaming, the understanding, the acting.

To begin with, the philosopher-executive is able to join his researchers in their dreams. It is mostly in dreams that one finds the delightful overtones that make life decorative, the ideals that spur man's efforts, the genial sensitivity to the nobler aspects of life, the soothing charm and heroic wit that cheer men's lives, the grace notes that beautify the theme of the laboratory, the glimpses of the ever-receding and reappearing patterns that fuse into the unity of the universe. Without dreams one is bound to the ordinary conventions of the waking hours. There is no inspiration. After all, are not scientific concepts but dreams petrified? Inability to dream strangles the source of the raw stuff of science.

In sharing the dreams of others, the philosopher-executive reveals a natural responsiveness through passive receptivity. He is the appreciative listener. As Walt Whitman has said: "To have great poets there must be great audiences too." He suspends knowledge and evaluation in his attention to the dreams of his scientists. A sympathetic ear has no diaphragm of discrimination. The very act of judgment implies a comparison and condemnation. When we condemn immediately, we think we understand the dream but we do not, and a separation has been induced between the judge and the judged. In place of judgment there must be an awareness, with no reference to particular standards, codes, or choices. The dream must be sensed as it is dreamt. If we let our experience and intellectual attitudes be deva sentries through which a proposal must pass before it receives an audience with our mind, we will never get a new idea. Every suggestion that conflicts with our past will be judged, condemned, and refused admission. The windowless wall of experience imprisons the rock-ribbed conservative, who mistakenly feels secure behind his own cult of the Ego. An executive should develop the state of self-forgetfulness and purge away every taint of self-consciousness. This will enable him to let go of himself and latch on to the dreams of others. He should not emulate that self-oriented character in Hawthorne's story, *The Intelligence Office*, who is continually crying out, "I want my place, my own place, my proper sphere, my thing to do, which nature intended me to perform when she fashioned me thus awry and which I had vainly sought all my life."

Dreams fall upon the mind of the philosopher-executive like a scene upon a clear mirror. Only after they have been given the freedom of their full impact is his entire experience, including the dream, conjured forth in a novel totality. In this way the dream does not become merely an accretion to experience like a barnacle to a ship. It is assimilated in a recasting of the entirety into a fresh harmony.

To share the dreams of creative artists requires a sympathetic appreciation of their strong leanings and idiosyncracies. Some are self-centered and conceited; some are naïve and intolerant of the practical; but all have a talent for creativity. The wellsprings of their dreams lie in their passions, instincts, and desires. These cannot be suppressed, for the source will soon be clogged by frustration and only nightmares sputter forth through the cracks and fissures. In short, the philosopher-executive loves people, not books, figures, rules, and charts. His feelings are identified with his neighbor's. He shares the sentiments of Su Tung-po, who, returning home one New Year's Eve after presiding over a court trial of prisoners arrested for salt smuggling, composed the following poem:

> On New Year's Eve, I should go home early,
> But am by official duties detained.
> With tears in my eyes I hold my brush,
> And feel sorry for those in chains.
> The poor are trying to make a living,
> But fall into the clutches of the law.
> I, too, cling to an official job,
> And carry on against my wish for rest.
> What difference is there between myself
> And those more ignorant than I?
> Who can set them free for the time being?
> Silently I bow my head in shame.

In his no-knowledge, the philosopher-executive does not seek perfection among his associates. He recognizes the slimy trap of harping on deficiencies. He understands the simple truth that mortals are full of defects. Criticizing the obvious lends neither prestige to the critic nor aid to the recipient. He remembers the Confucian comment to the effect that when you see a good man emulate him, but when you see a bad man examine your own heart. This does not mean that the philosopher-executive goes about in a sackcloth or cloaked with a self-centered sense of holy duty toward others. He just goes about naturally, subconsciously extending understanding and sympathy without conscious effort. The selflessness of his self-forgetfulness is contrasted to the overt selflessness of others of exaggerated convictions.

Yet the philosopher-executive does not dream on forever. He comprehends what lays down the rules of the game, what provides measure and taste, what limits are circumscribed for the scientific method, how they are influenced, what brings forth the endless series of opposing forces and compromises, and how close the total complex in reality can move toward the fantasy of the dreams. Dreams may wander beyond the bounds of rationality to bring back inspiring possibilities. But before they take form in the company's till, they must first put on the garb of realism. In the words of Emerson: "Of what use is genius if the organ is too convex or too concave and cannot find a focal distance within the horizon of actual life?"

It is the researcher's anxiety regarding the supervisor's appreciation of dreams that protests, perhaps in silence, against control by executives with inferior competence in the specialties. Latent in such an attitude is the implied sense of superiority in intellect and judgment by persons of those particular trainings. This narrow view is a misconception of the function of leadership. It is true that technical awareness of the subject matter is of great import as an ingredient of understanding. For this reason, the philosopher-executive has usually passed through the intensive period of a specialized discipline and attainment. He has an intimate feeling of the aspirations of the research mind. However, the astuteness of conducting esoteric research is not sufficient, nor for that matter necessary. It may be essential in the detailed guidance of others in the field. But overextended specialization may sever one's emotional link with society at large, leaving him progressively unable to sense the thoughts and motives of men in general. The responsibility of the leaders of research is to weld people of different talents and tempers into an integrated activity. Obviously the philosopher-executive cannot be a peer to the investigators themselves in the respective branches of science. He is, however, their superior in perspective, judgment, synthesis over a wider front of human interests, and understanding of Eliot's shadow, which falls

Between the idea and the reality
Between the motion and the act. . . .
Between the conception and the creation
Between the emotion and the response. . . .

To be practical is a matter of degree and relevance. Life on this planet, after all, is said to be good for only another two billion years. According to the best guess, at that time the sun will burst and the earth will turn into gas. If this long-range eventuality serves as the sole determinant to action, there is little reason for beautifying and improving man's world only to meet the incineration and gasification of all man's efforts. But reasonable living has an immediacy factor. There must be a recognition of the margin of error, the degree of elasticity, and the point of reference that govern each action. To be practical in terms of Shylock is to hoard; to be practical in terms of Senator Claghorn is to be elected; to be practical in terms of Attila the Hun is to plunder; to be practical in terms of St. Francis of Assisi is to love. If the point of reference is extended to ultimate questions, we have the philosophers of the classical tradition. If it is focused on forging a link between the immediate activity and an order of remoteness beyond that of common farsighted business, we have the philosopher-executive.

In the implementation of dreams, the philosopher-executive is infused with a love for learning. He recognizes the six "becloudings" of Confucius:

> You have heard the six becloudings? There is the love of being benevolent without the love of learning, the beclouding here leads to foolish simplicity. The love of knowing without the love of learning, whereof the beclouding brings dissipation of mind. Of being sincere without the love of learning, here the beclouding causes disregarding of consequences. Of straightforwardness without the love of learning, whereof the beclouding leads to rudeness. Of boldness without the love of learning, whereof the beclouding brings insubordination. The love of firmness without the love of learning, whereof the beclouding results in extravagant conduct.

The efficient management of organized research also demands gusto and quickened action. "He who would train in the fortress of contemplation," as the saying of Gregory the Great goes, "must first train in the camp of action." It is only in participation that the final synthesis of knowledge can be embodied in a unitary attitude to life. A faulty execution of a sound plan generates no more beneficial an outcome than a sound execution of a faulty plan. Some executives have even gone so far as to say that nothing is right which does not work. This may be too extreme a pronouncement. Yet, of what service to humanity is a dream entombed? Unless results are effected, the dreamer will continue to share the bewilderment of the March Hare, who was trying to fix the Mad Hatter's watch with butter in *Alice in Wonderland.* All he could say was: "And it was the *best* butter too, the *best* butter."

The art of getting things done involves the processes of making decisions and of doing. The goals of the parent concern must always be kept clear. Decisions must be made in their reflected light. The philosopher-executive knows what to do, when to do it, to whom to assign the task, and when to stop. Actions must be directional. The objective cannot be attained by flailing at generalities in a pointless dissipation of energy. The philosopher-executive heeds the ancient Persian proverb: "He who learns and learns and yet does not (take action on) what he knows is one who plows and plows yet never sows." Accordingly, if his parent organization is an industrial concern, his actions result in better products, increased consumer satisfaction, profits for investors, and improvement of the life of employees. If it is a government agricultural establishment, they lead to improved crops and animals, better farm practices, and benefit to the farmers, ranchers, and consumers. If it is a university, they stimulate scholarship in learning, integrity in beliefs, no-knowledge in feeling, and a humane vector in action.

The philosopher-executive also faces up to the problems of human frailties. He prunes the deadwood from the organization in such a fashion as to preserve equally the integrity of management and the respect for employees. He recognizes the captious power plays and wily pettifogging by that occasional unscrupulous minority. Wisely, he does not reciprocate in sly tactics and tricky circuities. He has learnt well the lesson about not wrestling with pigs: "You get dirty and they enjoy it!" For it has been said: "In shallow water dragons become the laughing stock of shrimps." Nevertheless, the philosopher-executive knows the ramifications of the circumstances and the effective means of dissipation of their damage.

In exercising sovereign prerogatives, the leader inevitably incurs the obstinacy and animosity of some associates. The same happens to the philosopher-executive, however altruistic he may want to be. He recalls that even the saints were not regarded as saints by all men. Otherwise, they would not have been stoned, crucified, and burnt. Confucius' advice to Tse-kung is well taken on this score. He was asked, "What would you say if all the people of the village like a person?" "That is not enough," answered Confucius, "it is better when the good people of the village like him and the bad people of the village dislike him."

The philosopher-executive recognizes that great works emanate from dedicated sincerity. If the creator is actuated by the will to goodness, he will untiringly pursue the hidden vagueness of unfinished experiments until he penetrates to the very heart of the problem. He will ferret answers from the far reaches of his mind. Ideas dredged from the very bowels of his soul are bound to bear the stamp of originality, for no two investigators are prototypes to such depths. He will also be impelled to communicate the fullness of his findings in the clearest expression so that others may be infected with the same enthusiasm and share in their use. When the lust for discovery is enkindled by quick adulation and quick gold, there will be trolling only in shallow waters. The fishing lines of these researchers cross each other. Concepts emerge entangled and similar; readers are barraged with hollow claims of priorities and enlarged snapshots of minnows of invention. The more insincere the researcher, the more puerile the emerging science.

Executives, too, need to be sincere. By sincerity the Taoist means a naturalness in no-knowledge. We cannot explicitly define such a state of naturalness. But we may look at what the Taoist calls the "pure men of old." Chuang-tze has spoken about them at length. A few representative snatches may provide a suggestive picture.

> The pure men of old acted without calculation, not seeking to secure results. They laid no plans. Therefore, failing they had no cause for regret, succeeding no cause for congratulations . . . So far had their wisdom advanced toward Tao . . . [they] slept without dreams, walked without anxiety. They ate without discrimination drawing deep breaths. For pure men draw breaths from their farthest depths; the vulgar only from their throats . . . [they] do not injure others but do not credit themselves with charity and mercy . . . They act differently from the vulgar but take no credit for their exceptionality . . . They appear to smile as if pleased, when actually it is but a natural response from the store of goodness within themselves . . . They appear to desire silence when in fact they had dispensed with language.

In his deep understanding of the interrelatedness of events and the nature of the minute seed that is destined for its matured expression, the philosopher-executive frequently implements the ultimate by injecting the early imperceptible germinal influence. He then lets nature with her many men of action develop the inevitable. One often wonders, for example, what would have been the present international picture had the Pope agreed to send the hundred learned scholars versed in the "seven arts" requested by Kublai Khan through Marco Polo in 1266.

Practically everything that has been written in this chapter so far can be derived from a common-sense approach. This is all to the good, for common sense is part and parcel of the suchness of nature that the Taoist stresses so much.

In addition, everything the philosopher-executive does "feels right." This "feel-rightness" is a common experience: the golfer who "senses" the perfect drive at the instant of contact of the club and the ball, the actor who "sees" that the audience is with him after his first lines, the lecturer who "is sure" his points are getting across, the negotiator who "knows" he is on the verge of a workable agreement. This "feel-rightness" has the quality of enduring. When things "feel right" there is a sense of enduring communication, of intimacy, of mutuality. A perfect communion with the suchness of nature provides the latent enduring which is not forced. All things fall into their proper places, so to speak. The philosopher-executive understands that all things do not fall into their proper places if some are left out, if some are distorted, if some are forced.

In many respects, the philosopher-executive is much attracted to Henri Bergson, as when he said in his letter to William James, "I saw to my great astonishment that scientific time does not endure . . . that positive science consists in the elimination of duration. This was the point of departure for a series of reflections which brought me by gradual steps to reject almost all of what I had hitherto accepted and to change my point of view completely." But then, Bergson's separation of scientific time from animate time and his stressing of pure dynamism and emphasizing that becoming is more of reality than that which becomes lead to a slight parting of the ways. The philosopher-executive, much as he appreciates becomingness, does not wish to be preoccupied with any one separate facet of nature at a time.

In many respects, the philosopher-executive is much attracted to

Alfred North Whitehead, as when he wrote, "In a certain sense, everything is everywhere at all times. For every location involves an aspect of itself in every other location." But then, Whitehead's fundamental rule ". . . that events have parts and that—except in a derivative sense, from their relation to events—objects have no parts" leads to a slight parting of the ways. The philosopher-executive does not wish to think in terms of "parts."

In many respects, the philosopher-executive is much attracted to George Santayana who attempted to develop a philosophical system out of many different alliances by "combining them as well as logic allowed without at heart ever disowning anything." Indeed, he is deeply sympathetic to Santayana when the poet-philosopher is accused of a lack of clarity. But then, Santayana's splitting up of his world philosophy into four realms leads to a slight parting of the ways. The philosopher-executive wonders how the four realms are fused. And why were there just four, anyhow? he asks himself as he muses over the infinite shades of nature.

In many respects, the philosopher-executive is much attracted to the worldly-wise philosopher, who recognizes the limitations of man and the practical realities of society and is satisfied with small increments of gain for the alleviation of human pain and the reduction of ignorance. But then, the well-intentioned vigorous pursuit of piecemeal attainments along a single or a few selected facets at a time leads to a slight parting of the ways. The philosopher-executive rather expects that restrictions to such approaches can but result in a disharmony in the whole.

Thus it is that the philosopher-executive shares much of the attitudes of many philosophical schools—but not completely. This indescribable residue after all the differences have been accounted for is the inspiration that the philosopher-executive derives from the ineffable continuum of nature, something pervasive, something enduring, the final presence of which enables him to "feel right" at each instant of action or inaction. And after the episode is past, everybody on the side lines will be able to sit back and say, with a certain degree of truth, "Why, that is just what *I* would have done. It is the *natural* thing to do."

In essence, the action of the philosopher-executive is guided by the proper pace of no-knowledge. Inwardly he cultivates spiritual enduring; outwardly he performs in social beneficence. He develops, in the phraseology of the old Chinese, "sageness within and kingliness without." The maintenance of this stature in his personage as a leader in society is his highest exemplification of responsibility.

Chapter 16

The Question of the Future

HAVING ESTABLISHED HUMAN-HEARTEDNESS as a point of reference for his motivations, the philosopher-executive observes that one of the chief questions confronting twentieth century science is: What, if any, should be the limits of scientific curiosity? This seems to be the question uppermost in the minds of men, who, while desirous of the benefits of science, shudder in their anxious moments at the possibilities of dreadful inventions along the way and of ultimate disaster if science is permitted to progress unfettered. The success of the philosopher-executive in dissolving the dilemma will determine the survival of science as we know it to be.

Actually, the bald question as stated is not a good starting point for resolution. This will be clarified later. Nevertheless this seems to be the form in which the problem is posed in the minds of many people. We should therefore first see what the picture looks like in its given form.

In the first chapter we described the science of today. She does not feel responsible for the ultimate applications and ramifications of her investigations. She forges ahead on all fronts willy-nilly. Her answer to the question we have raised seems to be: There are no boundaries circumscribing scientific research. It was this very attitude that led science quickly into her first crisis in the days of Galileo. Prior to that time the church considered *all* regions of human thought its own territory. The Scriptures were ordained the sole interpreter of all phenomena. When Galileo's observations disagreed with the church's explanation of the celestial orbits, his theory was challenged as a transgression of the spiritual domains of religion. Organized religion drew the line to science: "This far and no farther." The history of the resulting conflict and the subsequent emergence of science and decline of the church in the world of thought have been discussed in Chapter 14 and need no repetition here.

Generally speaking, there has been a surprising harmony since that period between science and religion through the gimmick of separating material from spiritual realms. With this convenient division of fields of inquiry into two blocs, one was recognized as the proper influential sphere of science and the other of religion.

From the Taoist viewpoint a separation of this kind is somewhat artificial. Solutions based on such an Aristotelian plus-or-minus classification are regarded as temporary expedients. The Taoist expects that the lease on time will eventually run out. A climax will occur if some overpowerful body of universal opinion stakes an arbitrary boundary of activity, even in "material" matters, beyond which science will not be permitted to trespass. If this happens, modern science will reach one of her greatest crises.

Up to now, the makeshift truce has been satisfactory. Limiting science to material matters during her early days presented as much freedom of action to science as if there had been no limitations at all. The horizon for investigative activities was almost infinite relative to the crudely developed instruments and techniques available to science at that time. In either case, science could have roamed at will without coming into frictional proximity to the claims of others. And this she did do.

In her fantastic progress, however, science rapidly strode across her initial fields of activities and before long stepped again beyond the line— this time with the Darwinian theory of evolution. Science's opinion rose in direct confrontation with that of established religion. The violent debate raged on for decades. Again it was resolved by invoking a separation of the realm of the body from that of the soul. Evolution of the body was agreed upon as a proper topic of conversation for science but evolution of the soul was considered to fall within the dogmatic purview of religion. In the main, science had won this round and peace was attained through a retrenchment of the sphere of influence of religion.

In recent years we have begun to see outlines of other threatening crises facing modern science. One of these indications was the conformity of genetic science with political ideology in Russia. The question of the effect of environment on the characteristics of an individual has become the center of a political-scientific controversy. The theory that hereditary traits are strictly transmitted through the germ plasm from one generation to the other and are not affected by the environment was considered contrary to the teachings of Marx and Lenin. Russian geneticists adhering to this school of thought were purged from their scientific positions of honor, although reinstated a decade or two later. Whether or not the germ plasm theory is correct is immaterial for the purpose of our thesis. The fact that one school of geneticists had successfully invoked compatibility with Communistic political ideology as a basis for selection over others shows the unquestioned ability of nonscientific forces to blunt the advance of science in her modern encounters with various segments of society.

People may argue that this single instance is not a valid example of the limited survival capacity of science in her present form. Indeed, American geneticists have stated eloquently that such a suppression of free science can occur only in a totalitarian country. They cannot imagine that such practices can possibly be condoned in this country. What was not made clear in their protestations, however, was the fact that the American geneticists were drawing the line on Russian political ideology: "This far (into the domain of science) and no farther." This reaction may be interpreted to be but the converse of the Russian political ideology drawing the line on genetic science: "This far (into the domain of Marxism) and no farther." But still, that can originate only in Russia, they say. So let us take another illustration, this time from the current annals of the United States.

The recent security hearing of one of the foremost American scientists is the case in point. A nuclear physicist was removed from his trusted position in the service of his Government. His case became a *cause célèbre* and the scientific circles in this country cried aloud against the judgment of the security committee. He had performed with distinction.

His potential contributions to the Government are enormous. He had not been disloyal. He had not broken security concepts in the sense that he transmitted classified information to unauthorized individuals. Yet his services with the Government were terminated on a security risk basis.

The question was not so much whether this great scientist was trustworthy in keeping the military secrets he had been privileged to know in his position. Instead the key issue was whether he is free to behave in his position according to his personal criteria of trustworthiness or whether he too must come under the general code prescribed by political officials. Scientists as a whole supported the physicist's philosophy. The Government decreed that the code of scientific self-determination must bow to the code of the Government in this instance. The security of the nation, as determined by nonscientists, is to supersede the security of individualism, as determined by scientists.

The important question for the purpose of this book is not which side is more morally justified. Rather the point we wish to note is: When science came into open disagreement with practices adjudged by duly authorized nonscientists to be necessary for the welfare of the country, science had to conform or retire from that society. In either case, science was forced to retreat and, for the time being at least, had to operate within a fenced area.

We observe, therefore, that within the last decade science experienced at least two instances in which powerful bodies of opinion in both hemispheres had told science: "This far and no farther." And in both instances, their decisions held and science backtracked.

In both recent episodes the outcome did not excite the masses of people as they followed the newspaper accounts. They failed to see any direct impact upon their daily lives. But it is conceivable that if science continues her rapid progress on the assumption of unrestricted boundaries and license, she will sooner or later begin to carve out areas in which people have deeply cherished untouchable interests. It is the painful feeling of uneasiness that somehow this may not be too far off that is disturbing to the laymen. Their imagination of the powers and intentions of science is being fanned by fantastic science fiction, TV, movies, comics, and news accounts. We may sketch three hypothetical lines of scientific progress to illustrate their subconscious fears.

Let us begin the first example with the very desirable research on a cure for cancer. Cancer, after all, is a form of disorderly rapid growth. It seems reasonable to assume that an understanding of the nature of growth may be a valuable starting point in the control of cancer. So the scientist begins to study how the normal cell enlarges, divides, and multiplies. He may want to begin his studies with the simplest cells and observe how they change in shape, size, number, and function. One of these is the fertilized egg cell. It is conceivable how this fertilized egg cell can be grown into a matured organism. A partial accomplishment has already been realized with plants beginning with a young embryo at the 32-cell stage excised from the seed and grown in a test tube. The 32-cell stage is only five successive cell divisions from the single-celled fertilized egg. In his reading the scientist notes that the stimulation of unfertilized animal eggs to divide in the absence of the sperm has been successfully demonstrated. Putting his imaginative two-and-two together, the scientist may be fascinated by the possibility: Will he be able to take an unfertilized human egg from the womb, cause it to divide in a test tube without the introduction of a sperm and grow it into a human being? According to conventional scientific parlance, this would be an intriguing challenge. And an "intriguing" or a "challenging" question is ipso facto sufficient ground for scientific forays; this is a natural consequence of the concept of the fenceless ranging of science.

If this sequence of events were to occur and reach a successful climax, the man in the street would be intimately involved in the distraught consequences. There would be no biological necessity for the male of the species. Sex becomes purely pleasure. Fathers would be as rare as drones after the maiden flight of the queen bee. Family life would no longer be the same. The summit of Huxley's *Brave New World* would be reached.

If this hypothetical sequence should occur or even so much as threaten to approach the climax of the single-sexed world, it would be quite understandable if the males of the world would rise in violent protest and light the hottest book-burning bonfire in the history of the world.

Let us begin the second example with the lie detector. It is a useful device. Many courts are considering it as admissible legal evidence. Efforts are in progress to improve its accuracy. As a matter of fact, the whole question of the transmission of messages is a thoroughly fascinating field of research. There are the high-speed computers and electronic relay systems capable of taking a prescribed set of thinking processes and applying it to various situations millions of times faster than the human mind. Mind reading has been a popular radio program in this country for a decade. Telepathy over a distance of thousands of miles has been claimed with an impressive array of supporting data.

These activities have excited great interest in the specific problem of thought transmission. Various laboratories are vigorously attempting to understand the underlying mechanism of extrasensory perception. Once embarked upon such a path the investigator will ultimately wind up, if successful, with mastering the art of mind reading. Since it is a common scientific practice to publish one's findings, before long there will be many people capable of reading the thoughts of others. How will the average man on the street react in a crowd of mind readers? Will the bride blush at her reception? How will the salesman make a living? How will a lawyer plead in court?

In this imagined progression, will science attempt to push the development to its bitter end? If so, how will the mass of people be moved to offset the threats to their most private of private possessions— their thoughts?

Let us begin the third example with the resuscitation of the heart during surgical failure. The alert surgeon has saved many a life on the operating table, when for some reason or another it has suddenly stopped beating. By rhythmic massaging, the heart can be made to function again after a lapse of several minutes. Other methods of resuscitation have also been highly effective in saving lives. Artificial respiration has revived individuals hours after drowning. The possibilities suggested by these practices have fascinated many a scientist. Studies have been described by a Russian investigator several decades ago in which the beating of the heart of a dog was restored twenty-four hours after it had ceased. If the dog was really dead, a technique of bringing an animal back from the grave has been demonstrated. About the same time, a well-publicized American researcher had also embarked upon experiments to revive the dead. Not only did he use animals, he even went so far as to test his technique on human bodies. What will be the consequences should these investigations result in the literal resurrection of human corpses? How will the zombies be regarded in the church, on the streets, and in the home. Will society condone the creation of Frankenstein monsters?

Admittedly, there may be some reductio ad absurdum in the three examples. But be that as it may—and we can add to the list other fantasies, such as tranquilizers, truth drugs, and other means of controlling human emotions—many people *do* feel considerable justification in such an extrapolative destiny of twentieth century science. Their fear has been aggravated by the obvious demand of science for absolute freedom in the seeking of scientific knowledge. Science is to wander unmolested forever onward. It would appear difficult for science to argue against the thesis that her present approach will ultimately lead to a direct contest with desires, forces, opinions, or institutions more powerful, more human, or more good (modern science being morally neutral) than herself.

Yet despite what may be imagined—and we view with considerable dismay the results of a recent nationwide poll by Purdue University indicating that over a tenth of the younger American students believe that there is something intrinsically evil about scientists—the scientist is actually a good and humble man. He recognizes that finite man can achieve only small increments of gains step-by-step in improving human welfare. Accordingly he tries to contribute to what he considers the maximum of his own capacity by intensive concentration on his own specialty in the natural sciences, leaving it to the social sciences and humanities to effect the humane integration of the laboratory findings into social beneficence. As he observes the use to which his creations have been applied, however, he begins to note how far "behind" are the social sciences and humanities. He yearns for a "balance" between the social and the natural sciences. He hopes that the humanities in their progress will discover the answers to the dilemmas engendered by the output of his laboratory. So far his hopes have not been fulfilled. There is little reason to expect that the wide gulf between the independently progressing segments of human knowledge will be lessened by a continuation of this divided outlook on life. This book has described another viewpoint, another mood, a bit Orientalized, a shadow of the Tao.

We view the good life for the scientist as a stream of overlapping instants of totality in which the advancing infinitesimals of science are assimilated in the human-heartedness of life at all instants of time, in lieu of the current haphazard progression of scientific advances perhaps to be followed by stretches of human-heartedness. In this way, the portentous dilemmas are "de-existed" before the crises, and faith in the future is restored at all instants of the present.

List of Contributors

THIS BOOK IS YET ANOTHER illustration of the infinity of influences which shape any given event. The author merely happens to be a collating eddy of the myriad contributions to the current of the Tao. It is fitting, before we close these covers, that we pay acknowledgment to this thesis. There was my good father, Siu Yan; there is my good mother, Siu Kau; there is my good wife, I-lien; there was ever helpful Kau Yau King. There are the millions of ancestors. There are the thousands of kind relatives, patient teachers, warm friends, and cooperative associates, particularly the staff of The Technology Press, the staff of John Wiley and Sons, Miss Veronica Ruzicka, and the reviewers of this manuscript. There are the many learned strangers, such as the following, who have recorded their knowledge and sentiments for subsequent generations to assimilate:

Anderson, E., and E. Exman, *The World of Albert Schweitzer,* Harper, 1955.

Auden, W. H., *Collected Poetry,* Random House, 1945.

Barnard, C. I., *Functions of the Executive,* 1938, and *Organization and Management,* 1948, Harvard University Press.

Bergson, H., *Creative Evolution,* translated by A. Mitchell, Holt, 1911.

Bhagavad-Gita (written about 500–200 B. C.), translated by S. Prabhavananda and C. Isherwood, Harper, 1947.

Bredon, J., and I. Mitrophanow, *The Moon Year,* Kelly & Walsh, Shanghai, 1927.

167

The Tao of Science

Bridgman, P. W., *Reflections of a Physicist,* Philosophical Library, 1950.

Brinton, C., *Ideas and Men,* Prentice-Hall, 1950.

Burchard, J. E. (Editor), *Mid-Century: The Social Implications of Scientific Progress,* Technology Press, 1950.

Carnap, R., *Logical Foundations of Probability,* University of Chicago Press, 1950.

Cassirer, E., *An Essay on Man,* Yale University Press, 1944.

Chuang-tze (died 275 B. C.), translated by Lin Yu-tang, *The Wisdom of Lao-tze,* Random House, 1948.

Cohen, M. R., *A Preface to Logic,* Holt, 1944; *Reason and Nature,* Free Press, 1953.

Confucius (551–479 B. C.), translated by Lin Yu-tang, *The Wisdom of Confucius,* Random House, 1938.

Crane, L., *China in Sign and Symbol,* Kelly & Walsh, Shanghai, 1926.

Croce, B., *Aesthetic,* translated by D. Ainslie, Macmillan, 1922.

Dampier, W., *A History of Science,* Macmillan, 1942.

Dewey, J., *Human Nature and Conduct,* Holt, 1922; *Reconstruction in Philosophy,* Beacon Press, 1948.

Durant, W., *The Story of Civilization,* Simon and Schuster, 1942–1953.

Eaton, G., *The Richest Vein,* Faber, 1949.

Eddington, A. S., *The Nature of the Physical World,* Macmillan, 1928.

Edman, I., *Arts and the Man,* Norton, 1939.

Einstein, A., *Out of My Later Years,* Philosophical Library, 1950.

Eliot, T. S., *Notes toward a Definition of Culture,* 1948, and *Complete Poems and Plays,* 1952, Harcourt, Brace.

Emerson, R. W. (1803–1882), *Works,* Houghton Mifflin, 1904.

Freud, S., *Civilization and Its Discontents,* Anglobooks, 1952.

Fromm, E., *Man for Himself,* Rinehart, 1947.

Fung Yu-lan, *A Short History of Chinese Philosophy,* Macmillan, 1948.

Grousset, R., *The Civilizations of the East,* Knopf, 1934; Introduction in *Art of the Far East,* Iris Books, 1950.

Hauser, A., *The Social History of Art,* translated in collaboration with S. Godman, Knopf, 1951.

Henderson, J. Y., and R. Taplinger, *Circus Doctor,* Little, Brown, 1951.

Herrigel, E., *Zen in the Art of Archery,* translated by R. F. C. Hull, Pantheon, 1953.

Hume, D. (1711–1776), *An Enquiry Concerning Human Understanding,* Oxford, 1927.

Huxley, A., *The Perennial Philosophy,* Harper, 1945.

James, W., *The Varieties of Religious Experience,* Longmans, Green, 1902.

Kakuzo, O., *The Book of Tea,* Dodd, Mead, 1906.

Kant, I., *Critique of Pure Reason,* translated by F. M. Müller, Macmillan, 1896.

Kenko, Y., *The Harvest of Leisure,* translated by R. Kurata, John Murray, 1931.

Keynes, J. M., *Treatise on Probability,* Macmillan, 1921.

Keyserling, H., *The Travel Diary of a Philosopher,* translated by J. H. Reece, Jonathan Cape, 1925.

Korzybski, A., *Science and Sanity,* International Non-Aristotelian Library, 1948.

Kramer, S. N., *Sumerian Mythology,* American Philosophical Society, 1944.

Langer, S. K., *Philosophy in a New Key,* Harvard University Press, 1942; *Feeling and Form,* Scribner's, 1953.

Lao-tze (born 571 B. C.), translated by Lin Yu-tang, *The Wisdom of Lao-tze,* Random House, 1948.

Lin Yu-tang, *The Importance of Living,* John Day, 1937; *The Wisdom of China and India,* Random House, 1942.

Li Po (701–762), translated and edited by S. Obata, *The Works of Li Po the Chinese Poet,* Dutton, 1922; A. Waley, *The Poetry and Career of Li Po,* Macmillan, 1950.

Lucretius (99–55 B. C.), *Of the Nature of Things,* metrical translation by W. E. Leonard, Dutton, 1921.

Malraux, A., *The Voices of Silence,* translated by S. Gilbert, Doubleday, 1953.

Maritain, J., *Range of Reason,* Scribner's, 1952.

Mees, C. E. K., *The Path of Science,* Wiley, 1946.

Mencius (372–289 B. C.), in Creel, H. G., T. C. Chang, and R. C. Rudolph, *Literary Chinese by the Induction Method,* Vol. 3, University of Chicago Press, 1952.

Merton, T., *Seeds of Contemplation,* New Directions, 1949.

Montaigne, M. de (1533–1592), *Essays,* translated by C. Cotton, Boni, 1923.

Moore, C. A. (Editor), *Essays in East-West Philosophy,* University of Hawaii Press, 1951.

Mumford, L., *Art and Technics,* Columbia University Press, 1953.

Needham, J., *Science and Civilization in China,* Cambridge, 1956.

Niebuhr, R., *Faith and History,* 1949, and *The Nature and Destiny of Man,* 1951, Scribner's.

Northrop, F. S. C., *The Logic of the Sciences and the Humanities,* 1948, and *The Meeting of East and West,* 1950, Macmillan.

Nott, S. C., *Chinese Culture in the Arts,* Chinese Culture Study Group in America, N. Y., 1946.

Ortega y Gasset, J., *The Revolt of the Masses,* authorized translation, Norton, 1932.

Ouspensky, P. D., *A New Model of the Universe,* Knopf, 1934.

Panchatantra (written around 200 B. C.), translated by A. W. Ryder, University of Chicago Press, 1925.

Pascal, B. (1623–1662), *Pensées,* translated by W. F. Trotter, P. F. Collier, 1910.

Planck, M. K. E. L., *Scientific Autobiography,* translated by F. Gaynor, Philosophical Library, 1949.

Pushkin, A. S., *The Poems, Prose and Plays,* edited by A. Yarmolinsky, Random House, 1943.

Radhakrishnan, S., and J. H. Muirhead (Editors), *Contemporary Indian Philosophy,* Macmillan, 1952.

Russell, B., *A History of Western Philosophy,* 1945, *Human Knowledge,* 1948, and *Impact of Science on Society,* 1951, Simon and Schuster.

Ryle, G., *The Concept of Mind,* Barnes and Noble, 1949.

Santayana, G., *Life of Reason,* Scribner's, 1906; *Three Philosophical Poets,* Harvard University Press, 1910; *Realms of Being,* Scribner's, 1942.

Schilpp, P. A. (Editor), *Philosophy of George Santayana,* 1940, *Philosophy of Bertrand Russell,* 1951, and *Philosophy of Sarvepalli Radhakrishnan,* 1952, Tudor.

Sorokin, P. A., *Social Philosophies of an Age of Crisis,* Beacon Press, 1950.

Su Tung-po (1036–1101), biography and translations in Lin Yu-tang, *The Gay Genius,* John Day, 1947.

Suzuki, D. T., *Studies in the Lankavatara Sutra,* Routledge, 1930; *Living by Zen,* Perkins, 1949; *Essays in Zen Buddhism,* Harper, 1949.

Tagore, R., *The Religion of Man,* Macmillan, 1931.

Tolstoi, L., *What Is Art?,* Oxford, 1898.

Veblen, T., *The Theory of the Leisure Class,* Vanguard, 1926.

Waley, A., *Three Ways of Thought in Ancient China,* Allen & Unwin, 1939.

Weber, M., *Essays in Sociology,* translated by H. H. Gerth and C. W. Mills, Oxford, 1946.

Whitehead, A. N., *Aims in Education,* Macmillan, 1929; *Essays in Science and Philosophy,* Philosophical Library, 1948; *Science and the Modern World,* Macmillan, 1948.

Wiener, N., *Cybernetics,* Technology Press and Wiley, 1948; *The Human Use of Human Beings,* Houghton Mifflin, 1954.

Index

Index

Being, 135
Bell Laboratories, 24
Benet, 93
Berenson, 47
Bergson, 102, 156
Bible, 8, 9
Bidwell, 13
Bill of Rights, 102
Biology, origin of, 142
Birth, 27
Bismarck, 96
Bohr, 104
Bolzmann, 30
Book of History, 146
Boyle, 9, 12, 20
Boyle's law, 52, 53
Brahma, 88
"Branch occupation," 117, 118
Brave New World, 163
Bridgman, 19, 30, 33, 51, 70
Brooke, 48
Bruno, 44
Buddha, 56
Buddhism and Buddhists, 21, 73, 77, 96
Buddhist Masters, 93, 96
Buddhist School of the Middle Path, 21
Bull of Heaven, 19
Burchard, 110
Butterfield, 104

Calendar, Gregorian, 55
    Julian, 55
Cancer, 163
Cardozo, 43
Carnap, 49
Carothers, 24
Cassirer, 46, 84
Castle, The, 103
Categories, 32, 33
Cause and effect, 27, 28, 32, 135
    Hindu version of, 27
Centrality, 126
Centralization versus decentralization, 122, 123, 124
Centralizing influence, 131
Ceremonies, 97

Cervantes, 9
Cezanne, 44, 46
Chang, 76
Charles I, 101
Chekhov, 66
Chesterfield, 55
Chesterton, 137
Chi-tsang, 21
Christ, 82, 144, 149
Chuang-tze, 17, 82, 97, 124, 132, 155
Chung, 126, 127
Churchill, 122
Cicero, 108
Civilization, disintegration of, 143
Clark, 13
Classification, 61
Clifford, 34
Coleridge, 72
Color, 88
Columbus, 13
Common sense, 43, 44, 156
Computers, high speed, 163
Concepts, 18, 19, 20, 22
    formulation of, 24, 25, 39
    usefulness of, 22
Conflict in codes, 149
Confucius, 82, 125, 130, 139, 151, 153, 155
Copernicus, 20, 96
Cost of Living, 85
Council for Financial Aid to Education, 86
Council of Nicaea, 110
Creativity, 5
    and courage, 90
    limitations on, 110
    and no-knowledge, 78
    and orthodoxy, 128
    and rationality, 78
    wellsprings of, 151
Crimean War, 65
Croce, 20
Cro-Magnon, 5
Crusades, 94
Cuneiform tablets, 6
Curriculum, 91, 92
Cyrus, 65

Index

Index

Index

Index